CLASSES:
A Marxist Critique

THE REYNOLDS SERIES IN SOCIOLOGY

Larry T. Reynolds, *Editor*

by **GENERAL HALL, INC.**

CLASSES:
A Marxist Critique

PAUL KAMOLNICK

Florida State University

GENERAL HALL, INC.
Publishers
5 Talon Way
Dix Hills, New York 11746

CLASSES:
A Marxist Critique

GENERAL HALL, INC.
5 Talon Way
Dix Hills, New York 11746

Copyright © 1988 by General Hall, Inc.

Publisher: Ravi Mehra
Consulting Editor: Anant Shina
Composition: *Graphics Division,* General Hall, Inc.

LIBRARY OF CONGRESS CATALOG CARD NUMBER: **88-82175**

ISBN: 0-930390-84-9 [cloth]

Manufactured in the United States of America

In memory of my father Sidney and,
for my mother Marion,
a shining sun for all who know her.

CONTENTS

Foreword

Paul Kamolnick offers in this monograph a very close, very critical reading of Erik Wright's *Classes.* The critique is vigorous, sharply pointed, unrelenting—all to an extent that some may feel exceeds customary standards. Clearly it is polemical, unabashedly so, and that may trip some wires in the reception of Kamolnick's argument. But its spirit is intendedly beneficent. Criticism, though its propriety has been restricted ever increasingly during the last three hundred years to domains of the literary, interrogates an activity, any activity, as to its conditions and possibilities. And in so doing, criticism's inescapable act of affirmation is also, inseparably, a "disputation of errors"—that is, polemical. A question always to be asked both in and of criticism is, how to discriminate error from that which is not error? . . . by what "criterion," and what do we purchase with it? This question circulates throughout Kamolnick's reading of *Classes,* both as surface thematic and as major undercurrent. The question is always on the verge of being redomesticated by the habits of the very activity to which it is put; after all, those habits are in significant measure *ours* (Kamolnick included). The sting of polemic keeps us alive to the question that is being asked, not only at the surface but also as major undercurrent.

While the title of Kamolnick's monograph is suitably descriptive, his thesis has more than Wright's book as its concern. Indeed, *Classes* figures in the main as a token for a much larger movement: renewed efforts to make (or remake) Marx useful to and for the interests of a social science that still struggles in the bowels of Kant's Third Antinomy. There is bound to be a remaindering in such efforts of normalization, for insofar as the interests of the one and other differ at root, making Marx useful to our social science will amount to radical translation. It may well be a "creative treason," as Robert Escarpit said of the practice of literary revivals; nevertheless the product that issues from the normalizing operation will be not Marx but a "sociologized Marx." Kamolnick strives to challenge that product, through the example of *Classes.* Of course, reproductions (i.e., productions) of arguments under the apparently constant presence of a name ("Marx," "Marxism," etc.) can occur only within and from contingent conditions of production. The appearance of the name as temporal continuity misleads. So, in challenging a sociologized Marx, through the example of *Classes,* Kamolnick necessarily works from the interest of another Marx, but this interest is not restorative of 1844 or 1867, nor of 1922 or 1967. To be sure, because Kamolnick's other Marx is formulated oppositionally, it cannot entirely escape the limits of that which it opposes. The interest of his argument would prefer not to conjure up the spirits of the past to its service, borrowing from them their names and battle cries and costumes. Yet, like the habits of Baudelaire's painter of modern life (in 1863), the habits of our practice of authority tend to be retrospective.

Part of the background to Kamolnick's larger focus on practices of a sociologized Marxism is composed by the disposition of sociology, an historically contingent academic discipline, to "sociologize the universe" (including sociology itself). Its efforts to integrate among its regulative oppositions a "hermeneutic of suspicion" has meant a divided reception of "Marxism(s)": on the one hand, an "object of inquiry," consisting of political-economic ideology, more or less concordant political-economic movements, and so forth; on the other hand, an especially strong "resource statement" of a hermeneutic of suspicion, one that recommends what has come to be called a "strong program of the sociology of knowledge." All the while, of course, the discipline of sociology struggles to keep the "unmasking turn of mind" turned outward, away from itself (thus marking the limit of its propensity to sociologize the whole). A sociologized Marxism has been ostensibly the goal of a mission—episodic in velocity, partly in correlation with degrees of academic risk-taking—to save "the scientific-rational part" of Marxism from its "ideological part." But in fact the goal (a sociologized Marxism) of that mission is already constituted as its premise, for sociology looks upon Marx, sees Marx, understands Marx, through its own lens. The Marxism that it would remake to its own proprieties is already made as such in the Marxism that it constitutes as "material" for sociologization. Why? Because, Kamolnick argues, Marx's argument and sociology's argument are radically different practices, and the former threatens at root the authority of the latter. The premises of sociology sociologize the radical difference that threatens—i.e., normalize it as "the ideological part" of a now already sociologized Marxism. There is nothing conspiratorial in that; it is simply inherent to the normality of sociology and of our social science generally. For sociology, a "Marxian sociology" is no more oxymoronic than a "Weberian sociology."

The *relata* of Kamolnick's opposition, "Marx's argument versus sociology's argument," are complex formations, no doubt. To say that at root they are different practices (the implication being that the radical difference ramifies throughout those complexities), and then to leave it at that, is hardly an act of clarity. While I will not attempt to summarize all of Kamolnick's claim, a very brief accounting of some "components" of the difference may be useful for purposes of orientation by preview. The question here is not of reasons but of specification: "in what ways" are Marx and sociology radically different, even contradictory, practices?

   • One regards knowledge (whether scientific or not)
   as a contingent production like any other production;
   the other, for all the universalizing thrust of its mis-

sion to sociologize, ultimately regards the governing principle of knowledge-seeking as exceptional.

• One makes its objects — and with that, itself — in the act of producing a practice of life; the other finds its objects outside itself, awaiting contemplation of their meaning (whether the contemplation be observational, experimentational, or by other instrumentality).

• One is prospective and *poietic,* taking its poetry from a future; the other is retrospective and *mimetic,* taking its measure from the presencings of a world already there, cut and dried.

• One is *not* science, i.e., not the historical formation that slowly developed during the sixteenth and seventeenth centuries and then began to flower profusely — though its own formation was surely not independent of that fecundity in the Enlightenment project; the other *is* science — or strives mightily and sometimes worriedly to be, despite Kant's "proof" that it could only pretend to that status.

Given such difference, not just quantitative but qualitative, it is hardly surprising that certain "aspects" or "components" of the complexities of the one would be by the other regarded as (indeed, would *be*) "ideological."

Kamolnick's larger argument is composed both of and in that difference. The aim is not to construct a bridge across the difference, thereby connecting Marx and sociology in some "more authentic" or "mutually faithful" way, for the two are *already* connected in the constitutive relationality of their opposition. Nor is the aim to build out of that opposition an eclecticism that would somehow, by extracting "correct parts" from each of the *relata,* transcend the opposition. Rather, the aim consists in an interrogation of the conditions and possibilities of the relationality at the site of its production, the labor process, without privileging the interrogative act as exceptional to that process. What is at issue there, in that process, is a structure of domination: one that is synonymous with the modern order, one from which our social science borrowed its authority, one that is being more and more rapidly dispersed in the making of a polyvalent, polyversive, decentered, though not to say domination-free, world. One of the ironies that circulate with the question of critique in the undercurrent of Kamolnick's argument is that, because of the universalizing thrust (i.e., because of the structure of domination whence the borrowed authority), our social science and sociology most especially had assumed at least until very recently that its operation (and demand for results of its operation) worked independently of its object of inquiry, a changing world. Kamolnick argues that such assumption has been sustainable in the practice of social science only insofar as that practice has been rhetorically successful in claiming for itself an exceptionality vis-a-vis the labor process. *Classes* is in some ways an especially striking study in the diminished persuasional capacity of that claim.

What I have said in description of Kamolnick's book may seem to overburden it with an argument too large and complex to be conducted satisfactorily within the confines of a small book, one that on its face modestly announces itself to be simply a reading of another book. To his credit, Kamolnick resists the temptation to change registers, preferring to keep the thematics of his book close to those of Wright's. While *Classes* does figure chiefly as a token, it is a token that appears on nearly every page of this book, and Kamolnick explicitly argues his tenacious critique from within the activity of *Classes*. But because the surface thematics of Kamolnick's book both are and are not those of Wright's book—the aim of the former is not simply to do better what the latter attempted—it is clear that the critique is situated in and guided by a larger argument. In his last chapter Kamolnick systematically sketches some aspects of this argument. It is, as he acknowledges, only a beginning. One would hope that this small book, Kamolnick's first publication (a revision of his master's thesis, moreover), is only his beginning.

Lawrence Hazelrigg

Preface and Acknowledgments

Written to bring his new data set to bear on his then quite familiar argument on the U.S. class structure, Erik Olin Wright's *Classes,* originally scheduled for publication in 1981 but actually published in 1985, was supposed to be a totally different production. Wright's "contradictory locations within class relations" concept had been the mainstay of his argument from the time of his major published work in *New Left Review* in 1976, on through his two books embodying this argument *(Class, Crisis and the State* and *Class Structure and Income Determination),* and culminating in a 1982 *American Sociological Review* article entitled "The American Class Structure." In *Classes,* Wright would attempt to parade the fruits of several years of lavish grant monies in the form of a transnational comparison of class structures and at the same time verify the explanatory potential of his concept of class structure.

Things did not go exactly as planned. Wright hints in the book's Preface about the reasons for postponing the book's appearance – fatherhood, death of beloved ones, and other major life experiences – but there were other perhaps more important reasons. Wright's succumbing to John Roemer's critique was certainly a turning point. The history of the unpublished manuscript, "What Is Marxist and What Is Neo- in Neo-Marxist Class Analysis?" traces this crisis-embellished period of Wright's argument. The second pre-Roemerist draft of this manuscript (April 1983), written with an eye to being incorporated in *Classes,* used Wright's "contradictory locations within class relations" concept and "verified" it with the use of

1

this new data set. The final draft, however, contained a remarkable Postscript in which Wright (1983b) claims the following:

> This paper was written in the Spring of 1983. In the six months since then I have undertaken a fairly thorough rethinking of my previous work on class structure. As a result of this "self criticism," I now feel that in certain important respects my earlier formulations were faulty, and as a result my strategy of class structure analysis needs to be transformed. In this brief postscript I cannot hope to lay out in detail these criticisms or the new strategy which I am pursuing, but I would like at least to indicate the central contours of the issues. (P. 249.)

Wright continues:

> It was only after an extended engagement with the theoretical work of the economist John Roemer [1982a, 1982b], particularly on the concept of class and exploitation, that I felt the necessity of trying to rethink the strategy....(Ibid., 250.)

Amazingly, Wright would now attempt to salvage *Classes* by basically rewriting it to accommodate both this "new" concept of class structure (taken more or less directly from Roemer) and his new data set. In the end, Wright's new transnational empirical data have been used to verify both concepts of class, the old one (i.e., in his 1982 *ASR* article and second and final drafts of the above-mentioned manuscript) and the new (see Wright 1984, 1985b).

For persons who had become familiar with Wright's argument on class structure analysis, the argument in *Classes* may have come as a surprise. Not only does it seem to mark a distinct break with his earlier argument, but Wright's sudden conversion to

"Roemerism" appears to have led to a wholesale abandonment of the capitalist labor process as the central determinant of class relations.

One of the central themes of this critique, however, is to focus on how this is *not* the case. Erik Wright's Marxism and practice of class structure analysis have a tremendous continuity if grounding is sought in Wright's own social formation within academic sociology and Althusserian Marxism. Wright's present argument is already implicit in Wright's (1976a) critique of Poulantzas. While *Classes* bears all the signs of a defensively constructed text written in the context of a major "crisis" in Wright's previous argument on class structure, the general contours of his argument have remained the same. How is this so?

Wright's "Class Boundaries in Advanced Capitalist Societies" (1976a) while received as a novel, empirically based contribution to a Marxist class analysis of modern capitalism, already prefigured the explicit conservatism that remains a major feature of his class structure analysis. An important footnote in "Class Boundaries," and later in *Class, Crisis and the State* (Wright 1979a), indicates the self-imposed superficiality of Wright's argument against Poulantzas. It is very important to understand that it is precisely Wright's failure to grapple with Marx's (or even Poulantzas's) argument regarding a class' conscious being (i.e. class struggle, class formation, etc.) that left Wright so wide open to non-Marxist critiques of the theorization of agency explicit and implicit in the work of Althusser and his influential followers (e.g., Poulantzas):

> This assessment of Poulantzas' analysis of classes will focus on the actual criteria he uses to understand classes in contemporary capitalism, *rather than on the epistemological assumptions which underlie his analysis. I will thus not deal with the problem of his general concept of "class struggle" and his categorical rejection of "consciousness" as a*

useful category in a Marxist analysis. While it is important to deal with these issues (indeed, most reviews of Poulantzas' work are preoccupied with these questions rather than the substance of his argument), I feel it is more useful at this point to engage Poulantzas' work at a lower level of abstraction. (Wright 1976, 13; 1979a, 43-44. Italics added.)

By not critically engaging the fundamental philosophical and methodological assumptions grounding Poulantzas's then recently published book *Classes in Contemporary Capitalism,* Wright restricted his analysis of classes to one over boundary criteria. In *Classes,* unsurprisingly, this remains the case.

As I argue in chapter 2, Wright's present reliance on so-called methodological individualism and its "rational actor" premised in "game-theory" for grounding the construction of his dependent variable "class attitude" can hardly be considered a Marxist preoccupation with the epistemological category of consciousness. In fact, Wright does not once discuss Marx's critique of precisely this kind of abstract bourgeois liberalist premise, nor Marx's broader argument grounding a class' conscious being. Wright's recent "turn" and apparent preoccupation with consciousness is not grounded in a Marxist materialist debate over the practice of class consciousness in a so-called class analysis, but in a liberalist bourgeois philosophical critique of functionalist explanation in social theory.

The basic objective of this critique is to construct an immanent argument against Wright's *Classes.* Rather than accept his practices of consciousness, class struggle, and subject-object relations, however (as Wright has done in his critiques of Poulantzas), these practices serve as a point of departure for my broader critique of Wright's class structure analysis.

My construction of a critical argument against Wright is produced in the following manner. In chapter 1, I argue that a sociologized variant of Marxist practice is the uncritical presupposition of Wright's class structure analysis. Furthermore, far from challenging this practice, Wright's Althusserian and "post-Althusserian" influences have served to buttress it. I will suggest that the production of this variant of Marxism implies an acceptance of a metaphysical materialism at odds with a Marxist materialism. More specifically, I establish that a specific appropriation of Marx's legacy has been produced by Wright, and at the heart of this variant of Marxist practice lies a particular practice of the labor process. Given this specific practice of labor and the labor process, I then argue its implications for the production of Wright's specific argument on class structure analysis.

Chapters 2 and 3 produce the main arguments against *Classes*. In chapter 2, I claim that Wright's practice of consciousness and class consciousness leads not to a knowledge of class structure but to a radical epistemological relativism that, by necessity, actually undermines the possibility of Wright's knowledge of class structure. This radical relativism cannot be overcome within the terms of Wright's argument grounding class consciousness. Fundamental problems in Wright's practice of objectivity and objective interests also are addressed and are linked directly to Wright's neo-Kantian grounding.

The basic objective of chapter 3 is to demonstrate how Wright masks this relativist predicament, and necessarily so, through the authority and use of a particular practice of *scientific* method. I argue that Wright must revert to what amounts to a special theory of the labor process (along with its accompanying special agent and products) in order to overcome the problems plaguing his principle of subjectivity in chapter 2.

Wright's attempts to demonstrate (1) the uniqueness of scientific concepts; (2) a boundary constraining and defining the "conceptual" and the "empirical"; and (3) specific "conceptual constraints" on the production of "his concept" of class structure are challenged. I argue that Wright's failure to defend these grounds implies the impossibility of defining "his concept" of class structure and reproduces the terms of epistemological relativism.

Chapter 4 consists of two parts. First, I draw out the general implication of my critique for Wright's specific practice of empirical investigation. Although Wright has not established a consistent grounding for the so-called empirical investigations to be found in chapters 5, 6, and 7 of *Classes,* he nevertheless proceeds to "verify" his concept of class. I argue that the problem of empirical investigation, as Wright sees it, is a false problem, since Wright has failed to specify the conditions under which such an investigation could be both possible and meaningful.

Not only does this critique have specific implications for Wright's practice of empirical investigation, it has implications for the very directions a Marxist class analysis should take. The remainder of chapter 4 deals with what I take to be more promising directions for Marxist class analysis. The thrust of my argument centers on a fundamental reorientation to the practice of the labor process—one that makes class analysis itself internal to class formation and the class struggle. Instead of the "class structure" being an object of analysis, and "analysis" being a procedure for specifying abstract properties of this "structure," class structure analysis itself must be practiced as the process of making the class struggle. This alternative practice of class analysis and its implication for current sociologized Marxism are developed by focusing on the radically different practices of subjectivity, objectivity, knowledge production, science, empirics, and dialectics that ground each practice as both textual and nontextual objectification of the class struggle.

Wright's Marxism, and this is the major point of this critique, is an example of a Marxism no longer critical (if it ever had been) of the very basic foundations of neo-Kantian social science. Practices of the labor process, objectivity, knowledge production, and science receive their warrant from standard non-Marxist sociological methodology. Marxism's very practice within the social formation of present-day academic social science is conditioned on the possibility that professional sociological standards are reproduced. Hence, Wright's so-called Marxist sociology turns out to be no more than a subset of sociological theory more generally. Marx has become a sociologist, and Marxist class analysis another set of theoretical hypotheses to be confirmed with the use of mainstream academic authority. Rather than embark on the much-needed challenge of overthrowing the false practice of present-day sociology, Wright has conflated Marxism with sociology's very condition. There is no way of escaping the necessity of immanent critique, yet Wright, because of his stake in the present regime of academic sociology, has mostly failed even to pose this question.

I would like to acknowledge those most involved in the production of this critique. First, I would like to acknowledge Lawrence Hazelrigg as a principal and most critical influence in the production of this work. His practice of Marx's argument as a critique of neo-Kantian sociology, great sense of humor, and general support and encouragement for activist graduate students has proven invaluable to my own formation. I would also like to acknowledge Larry Isaac for his always sensitive, sacrificing approach toward students and for the countless hours we have spent cutting through "neo-Marxism" to get at a truer Marxist practice of the labor process. I would like to thank the graduate students in the Department of Sociology at Florida State University for the many long hours of discussion, polemics, and critical argumentation. Though I retain sole responsibility for this printed text, the many arguments practiced throughout have certainly benefited from the numerous critical exchanges and countless patient (and not so patient) sessions endured by my student friends. And finally, I want to express my gratitude and love to my wife Moni for helping to make our relationship both a radical crucible for ongoing socialist work and a living expression of passionate commitment.

Chapter 1 A Critique of Erik Olin Wright as a Critique of Sociologized Althusserian Marxism

A critique of Erik Olin Wright's *Classes* should be simultaneously understood as a broader critique of a sociologized version of Marxism. Wright's version of this sociologized Marxism, produced within an academized Western practice of Marxism, is in fact a contemporary example of what Marx termed "contemplative materialism," which is in actuality a form of idealism.[1]

My critique, however, unlike Marx's assault on the liberalist–Enlightenment grounded nineteenth-century practices of his time (e.g., political economy, philosophy, political theory), is part of present-day attempts to practice a truer Marxist sociology.[2] In this chapter I attempt to sketch out some of the major practices shaping Erik Wright's practice of Marxism. In short, I lay the broader grounding for my critical arguments in subsequent chapters that Wright's failed class analysis is rooted in (1) his failure to practice a truer practice of the labor process (process of historical self-objectification) and (2) that this false practice of the labor process is itself grounded in Wright's social relation as a neo-Kantian academician.

Wright's relation has led to a reading and practice of Marxism that buttresses this academic distancing from class struggles. The relation of "class analyst," and its specific practice within a so-called Marxist sociology, has made a Marxist critique of the capitalist labor process conditional on whether it reproduces the relation of this analyst. Wright's book *Classes* must be understood as an objectification that relies exclusively on this bourgeois academic authority and presupposed labor process.

Marxism, as a revolutionary critique of the historical formation of bourgeois capitalist commodity production, is also itself a historical formation. In other words, Marxism is both a historical production within determinate conditions and a critique of such conditions. Marxism as an objectivity, as an actual historical production, is itself an objectification of objective activity. To speak of Marxism is to speak of a historical formation of practices that have been produced through the very development of bourgeois social relations. The implication being that practices of Marx's texts and legacy can never resort to some privileged location that somehow transcends this historical self-objectification. Any practice of Marxism must be grounded thoroughly within the historical production of capitalism and, especially for the twentieth century, the production of capitalist imperialism.

There have been several major practices of Marxism over the last hundred years, practices that themselves are inextricably linked to determinate conditions of objective historical activity. For the sake of historical illustration, not an exhaustion of "Marxism after Marx," let us consider some of the major practices of Marx's meaning. The social formation of the Second International was one such formation. The organization of the European proletariat in the latter third of the nineteenth century and the first decade of the twentieth into mass social democratic parties led to the production of several strategies for revolutionary work. Within Germany alone, Marxism had been read and practiced as both abandonment of revolutionary class struggle in favor of parliamentary majoritarian reformist socialism (Bernstein's critique) and the necessity to break with the "bourgeoisification" of revolutionary working-class organization (Luxemburg's critique). Both attempted to render Marx's argument one that justified the critique they were constructing concerning the practical conditions for overthrowing bourgeois capitalist social relations.

Even before the "Second Internationalization" of Marx it can be argued that Marxism had been transformed into a very different historical practice. Nascent neo-Kantianism, Darwinist naturalism, and the pietist/industrialist background of Engels himself led to the practice of Marxism as a naturalistic pragmatism. Marx's struggle against the Hegelian system and critiques of precisely the kinds of naturalisms that would later pass as Marxism were not even textually available for the first generation of Marxists in the 1880s and 1890s.

V.I. Lenin's critique of the Second International in its various forms marks another major historical practice of Marxism. While Marxists are certainly divided over the meaning and significance of Lenin's strategy of revolutionary work, there is no doubt that variations on Lenin's critique still have tremendous historical meaning for Marxists throughout the world, most especially for Marxists practicing under conditions of extreme police repression in underdeveloped dictatorial U.S. client-states (e.g., El Salvador, Chile, South Korea).

Leninist strategies of revolutionary work have also been historically crucial in the successful consolidation and defense of revolutionary anti-imperialist movements that have come to power under and continue to confront conditions of extreme counterrevolutionary violence (e.g., Vietnam, Cuba, Nicaragua). At the same time, the historical failure of non-Leninist social democratic strategies (e.g. Jamaica under Manley and Chile under Allende's Popular Unity) to defeat the counterrevolutionary class power of U.S. capitalist imperialism provides additional validity to Lenin's practice of the class struggle against imperialism.

Of course, Lenin's critique of imperialism is not the same thing as either Marx's critique or the social formation of the Third International (Comintern). And to a great extent this formation, Stalinized from 1923 to 1953, has had its vociferous critics as well. Some of these critics attempted to critique Stalinism from the standpoint of an "authentic" Leninism, which they saw as more compatible with "orthodox" Marxism, (e.g., Trotsky and the various Fourth Internationals, Gramsci's critique); others completely broke with Bolshevik strategy over the meaning of revolutionary work and organization in the twentieth century (e.g., Luxemburg).

The social formation of what has come to be called Western Marxism[3] has also had a decisive significance for the meaning and practice of Marxism. While there is no central principle guiding this Marxism, the failure to make twentieth-century European socialist revolutions, hostility to Leninism (and especially statist Stalinism) and the increasing academization and estranging disassociation of Marxist "theory" from the concrete conditions of revolutionary class struggle characterize the terrain of its practice. Not surprisingly, and paralleling this practical disassociation of Marxist "theory" from revolutionary class struggle, a reading and practice of Marx's argument has been produced that justifies this distance. The reduction of class struggles and the process of class formation to "intellectualized" isolated exercises in class analysis is one central feature of this Western Marxism. The grounding for such an analysis is sought, not in the conditions of revolutionary class struggle, but, on the contrary, in the non-Marxist philosophies and conditions grounding the practice of neo-Kantian based modern social science.

While Marxism has been and must remain a historical formation, this, after all, is the essence of revolutionizing practice; furthermore, real transformations in the labor process (e.g., its globalization) necessitate different strategies and tactics that transform this labor process, we may critique other Marxisms for failing to ground revolutionizing practice. In fact, when the label "Marxism" is associated with movements, regimes, practices, or strategies that do not illuminate but rather conceal or mask the concrete conditions of control over the labor process, we may say that they are false renderings of an actual labor process.

Marxism is true when it develops a truer practice of the process of self-objectification. For Marx, the question of *how* we make ourselves actual, real, objective, and within what process of historical social relations is what grounds truth. The question of truth is a question of how reality is made, since the meaning of reality is in the making of reality. A false practice of the actual process of historical self-objectification may be practiced as a "Marxism," but at the expense of a falsification of how reality is made. In this sense, there are and have been "Marxisms" that are true by virtue of being actualized historically as Marxism, but false to the extent that they mask/obfuscate/fetishize the real labor process.

In what follows I would like to argue briefly against what I consider some very important conditions that buttress the ultimately uncritical and false practice of the labor process at the heart of Erik Wright's Marxism, one that makes his Marxism incapable of producing a thoroughly revolutionary practice of the class struggle.

One crucial historical formation conditioning the production of Marxism, and most relevant for purposes of this critique, is that of modern bourgeois social science, most especially the neo-Kantian grounded discipline of academic sociology. It is within this historical domain that Erik Olin Wright is alleged to have made significant contributions to our understanding of social classes in advanced capitalist societies, as well as our understanding of "Marx's legacy." Let us first consider just how it is that Marxism has been conflated with bourgeois sociology's conditions of existence.

One of the most important means of conflating Marxism with present-day neo-Kantian sociology has been through the rewriting of Marx's historical significance, and most especially the terms of this rewriting itself. Two terms of this rewriting are of particular significance: producing a distinction between an

immature prescientific and a mature scientific Marx; and justifying the sameness of Marxism and sociology through a focus
on their respective objects and methods (rather than their *subject*) of inquiry.

The historians of sociologized Marxism (or Marxist sociology, as they are fond of saying) generally maintain a distinction
between an early, "not yet scientific" Marx and a later, thoroughly
scientific Marx, thus authorizing a rejection and expulsion of
this early Marx from their production of Marxism. The rejection
of the "early Marx" as unscientific seems to be aimed at making
Marxism a legitimate competitor within bourgeois sociological
practice. Of course there can be good grounds for critiquing
Marx's earliest works, from 1837 to 1844. The rejection of the
"early Marx" was carried out by Marx himself in his early
writings against the Hegelian school, Young Hegelianism, the
remnants of Kantianism in his own argument, and finally the
naturalism of Feuerbach. But the general thrust of at least some
of the historians of Marxist sociology (e.g., Bottomore, Flacks)
has not been to critique Marx's grounding in Hegelian philosophic
labor from a more concrete standpoint but to re-Kantianize
Marx's argument. The relationship of Marx to both Kant and
Hegel has tended to be read as a vindication of Kant (scientific
Marx) and a final defeat of Marx's bout with Hegelianism and
Young Hegelianism (early Marx).

Contrary to the official history of Marxist sociology, I maintain that Marx's deafening and fundamental criticisms of bourgeois sociology at issue here can and are to be found in Marx's
early texts.[4] Marx's critique of the abstract philosophical labor
at the heart of both Hegelianism (and Young Hegelianism) and
the abstract materialism of Feuerbach (and bourgeois liberalism
more generally) provides, explicitly and implicitly, the grounds
for an assault on the edifice of bourgeois social scientific authority
and practice. Furthermore, without a thoroughly critical reading
of Marx's early arguments, Marx's later texts appear as abstract,
self-contained works rather than more concrete and revolu-

tionary extensions of fundamental criticisms already at issue in Marx's early work.

A second form of rewriting Marxism as justification for sociologized Marxism is based on an assertion that Marxism and sociology share basically the same concerns. This alleged similarity stems from a comparison in terms of their respective *objects* and *methods* of inquiry.[5] The object of each is conceived as an abstract "social structure" consisting of various "processes" and "causal mechanisms," while the methods of Marxism and sociology are both allegedly directed toward producing "objective" knowledge of this social structure. Wright's demand for "objectivity" is here understood, as I argue throughout this critique, as a demand for a knowledge that is independent of any given historical, cultural particularities of the subject–theorist. The practice of "sociological methods" or "methodology," given this practice of "objectivity," is an attempt to efface subjectivity by bracketing historicity (controlling for "bias"). The claim of a special methodological practice of inquiry—whether quantitative, qualitative, historical, ethnographic, or any other kind for that matter—is simply a ritualistic procedure that even "Marxist sociologists" go through in order to eliminate their subjectivity–historicity as a precondition for knowing objectivity. It is practiced as the major precondition for generating true knowledges of "objective" social structures.

Given similar objects and methods of inquiry, the differences between Marxism and sociology are reduced (by the historians of "Marxist sociology") to differences of explanation *within* sociological theory. From this standpoint, so-called *Marxist sociological theory* is then alleged to consist of the principal claim that "class structure" and, more generally, "the economic structure" are principal causal forces in historical society. On the other hand, vis-a-vis fundamental causal processes, *non-Marxist sociological theory* is alleged to accept a premise of causal pluralism. The so-called research agenda that follows from such a self-understanding and practice of Marxism focuses on proving the primacy-determinacy of class structure and economic structure over other aspects of social structure. Of course, for "class analysts" of this "class structure," such as Wright, the task consists in demonstrating the superior explanatory capabilities of one concept of class over others (e.g., Wright's concept over that of Poulantzas).

Wright's practice of Marxism has its condition within bourgeois sociology and therefore has been transformed into a variant of sociological theory rather than a revolutionary critique of the conditions of such theory. The academic labor process practiced by neo-Kantian grounded mainstream sociological theory has replaced Marx's critique of such a labor process. To the great detriment of a more revolutionary Marxist practice, the historians of this "Marxist sociology" have systematically excluded this reading of Marx and have instead developed a more sociological and "scientific" Marxism appropriate for grounding their authority.

While academic sociology and bourgeois social science constitute the basic conditions for Wright's argument as a "class analysis" of "class structure," this is not the whole story. I alluded earlier in this chapter, and even signify in the chapter title, to the influence of Althusserianism for Wright's argument. But before considering Althusser's influence, a few words about Leninism and, more specifically, Communist party practice.

While it is undoubtedly true that Leninist-based Communist parties (in and out of power) have had tremendous historical significance for the shaping of revolutionary strategy, work and organization under conditions of capitalist imperialism, their meaning for practices of Marxism is by no means noncontroversial. On a more sympathetic reading, one I have alluded to earlier, a Leninist critique may be understood as a truer Marxist practice. "Truer" in the sense that the reality and actuality of the capitalist labor process as a global imperialist relation has transformed the meaning and objectives of revolutionary work. To the extent that Lenin correctly laid a foundation for organizing the working class into a decisive force that could confront imperialism on a global scale, we could argue that Lenin was indeed also a Marxist. And by implication, Leninists are indeed also Marxists.

There is another side to this controversy. The precise extent to which Leninism, or "Marxism-Leninism," acknowledges the concrete nature of the labor process and hence the implications that Leninist-based strategies of revolutionary work have for realizing the interests of the working class is one such controversy. The history of Stalinism, the various Soviet-led police actions designed to put down worker-based uprisings in Hungary, Poland, and Czechoslovakia, "intersocialist" wars and conflict (e.g., Sino-Soviet, Sino-Vietnamese), and the proliferating debates beginning in the early 1960s and radically picking up steam in the 1970s and 1980s within Eastern Europe, the Soviet Union, China, Cuba, and Vietnam over "economic reforms" indicate a different meaning for Leninism. A less sympathetic reading may even conclude that Leninism has ceased to express the concrete needs (if it ever even did) of the working class.

This controversy also engulfs what we mean by "reading Marx." What happens to Marxism when it is made conditional on what has come to be practiced as Leninism, Marxism-Leninism, or Communist party practice? Traditionally, Marxism is read as a doctrine that lays the necessary conditions for the authority of "the party" and the necessary leadership or "vanguard" role of the party in the construction of authoritative and legitimate practice. The question that arises is, How is Marx's argument read and practiced so that it buttresses such a Leninist practice? Which parts of his text are rendered significant, which are deemed inessential, and which are actually "read out" of Marx's legacy and replaced with more "appropriate" renditions of what Marx "really intended but did not say." Is it not actually the case that Marx's argument has been mostly replaced within Communist party orthodoxy by that of Engels and Lenin, and that authoritative "Dialectical Materialism" and "Historical

Materialism" are grounded far more in Plekhanov's pre-Marxist materialism than in Marx's argument? What happens to Marx's revolutionary criticism of capitalism and the liberalist social formation when its very existence is contingent on whether it produces/reproduces the authority of the Communist party and its "inevitable" role? How is Marxism made from within the institutional-historical conditions of Communist Party practice?

While there is not and can never be an "unconditional" and nonpremised "pure" practice of Marx's argument, the presentation of "the only real Marx" as the Marx that authorizes, theorizes, and makes inevitable the dominant role of the Communist party relies on such an ahistorical authority. The false presentation of the historical-particular as the natural-universal becomes a means of rewriting Marx's argument solely as a means of justifying current practice as necessary, and therefore critique of present practice as unnecessary.

The historical production of Marx's legacy as Communist party practice has certainly been of crucial importance to the struggle against capitalism (especially capitalist imperialism). Nevertheless, by making the reproduction of Communist party authority a historical condition of reproducing Marx's revolutionary criticism, different practices of Marxism, perhaps far more revolutionary, will necessarily be excluded. It has most certainly been the case that the publication of Marx's extremely important early writings over the last fifty years has provided the basis for revolutionizing officially practiced Communist party Marxism and, furthermore, that revolutionary critiques of alienated labor under "Actually Existing Socialism" will proceed in spite of, not because of, official Communist party "Marxism-Leninism."

In short, "Marxism-Leninism" may be false to the extent that the real conditions of the labor process are masked through Communist party practice. While Leninism has undoubtedly had (and will continue to have) a major impact on historical practice, its meaning vis-á-vis the concrete interests of the working class and the future of the very meaning of Marx remain open to debate. With the stage set, I would now like to return to the question of Althusser's relation to Erik Wright's practice of Marxism.

Following both the death of Stalin and the 20th party Congress of the Communist party of the Soviet Union (CPSU), major dissident, critical, and conservative currents within and outside the international Communist parties were "unleashed."[6] One of the most important—and for the purpose of critiquing Wright, *the* most important—was the work of Louis Althusser and his followers within the French Communist party (PCF). Althusserianism's subsequent major role in shaping the "debates" within British Marxism, especially the bitter cleavages surrounding editorial direction of *New Left Review,*[7] significantly shaped the direction of academic Marxism in the United States as well.

Though the meaning of Althusser's Marxism and exact nature of his critique has been the subject of much writing over the last twenty years, Althusser's defense of Leninist party orthodoxy is undeniable. And it was Althusser's continuous defense of what he took to be the necessary separation of philosophy (as embodied in the party and grounded in "materialist dialectic" or "dialectical materialism") from history (historical materialism) that authorized the very reading of Marx he was to produce. This was certainly not unique to Althusser's reading.[8] The vigor with which Althusser's arguments were put forward was tantamount to the admission that Leninism itself was at stake. In the wake of much criticism—from former disciples (e.g., Ranciere) and some of the British Marxists (e.g., John Lewis, E.P. Thompson)—Althusser reasoned:

> It is not too much to say that what is at stake today behind the argument about words, is *Leninism.* Not only the recognition of the existence and the role of

Marxist theory and science, but also the concrete
forms of fusion between the Labour Movement and
Marxist Theory, and the conception of materialism
and the dialectic. (Althusser 1976, 115.)

While Althusser was well aware of the criticisms leveled at
metaphysical practices of Marx's argument,[9] his argument in
defense of a "scientific-theoretical" reading of Marx was em-
phatic:

> Who, really, is naive enough to think that the ex-
> pressions: Marxist *theory,* Marxist *science* — sanc-
> tioned, moreover, time and time again by the history
> of the Labour Movement, by the writings of Marx,
> Engels, Lenin and Mao — could have produced the
> storms, the denunciations, the passions we have
> witnessed, if nothing had been at stake except a sim-
> ple quarrel over words. (Ibid., 114-115.)

One of the hallmarks of Althusser's reading of authoritative
Marxism (similar to sociologized Marxism generally) was the
denunciation of Marx's early texts as merely "ideological" or
"prescientific" and, based on this, an attempt to construct a particular practice of Marxism as "mature" science devoid of any of
the remnants of Marx's early arguments. As stated earlier, there
are very good grounds for critiquing Marx's early arguments on
account of their grounding in a still Hegelian practice of the
labor process. Nevertheless, by "reading out" this part of Marx's
argument altogether, works of extraordinary significance were
devalued (e.g., *The Economic and Philosophic Manuscripts of
1844*). In the 1844 *Manuscripts* in particular, Marx's critique of
alienated labor (the embryonic stages of the later argument in
Capital), reflections on the more general process of self-
objectification, and devastating critique of Hegel's entire
system developed positions that went far beyond any then avail-

able. By the time of the *Theses on Feuerbach* written in the Spring of 1845 Marx would undermine the very labor premise that to this day grounds contemporary social science and philosophy.

With Althusser's "structural Marxism" becoming a significant tendency among radical sociology graduate students in the mid to late 1970s, this practice of Marx's legacy became more widespread.[10] Far from Althusser's Marxism being placed within the context of the crucial events unfolding in Europe throughout the period of his developing argument (e.g., the Sino-Soviet split and Althusser's inclination toward Maoism, events in France both pre- and post-1968, the development of Eurocommunism), there was a strong tendency to abstract from these developments and fetishize Althusser's "scientific Marxism." Adding to the abstractness of Althusser's argument was the fact that the time lag between Althusser's publication in French and subsequent translation into English was several years.[11] Finally, and perhaps most important, despite Althusser's intentions, Althusser was read (constructed) by U.S. readers largely in a U.S. terrain of issues, debates, etc., that was obviously different from that in France. For example, Althusser's Marxism was read in the United States much more as a sociologized Marxism than it was in France.

Erik Olin Wright's sociologized Marxism, in addition to its grounding in bourgeois sociological theory, then, was produced as an extension of the "structural Marxism" of Althusser. Besides the obvious notoriety of Althusser and his most loyal disciples on the British Marxist scene, at least two reasons may be offered for the institutional presence of Althusserian Marxism in U.S. academic sociology. First, as a means of gaining entry into a discipline with social scientific pretensions, Althusserians were prepared to argue the superior scientific capabilities of "DIAMAT" grounded Marxism as against its bourgeois adversaries. Second, at least one prominent "neo-Marxist" has argued that "structural Marxism" was a convenient vehicle for Marxists to gain entry into a discipline already strongly structural-functionalist in orientation (Burawoy 1982, S18). The compatibility of Althusserian structural-functionalist DIAMAT with neo-Kantian structural-functionalist bourgeois stratification theory could be produced, since both in fact agreed on fundamentals concerning the role of theory construction and methodology in social scientific explanation. In this way, not only did some key radical journals become conduits for this variant of Marxist practice (e.g., *New Left Review, Insurgent Sociologist, Kapitalistate*) but mainstream sociological journals did to some extent as well.[12]

Wright was also involved, as students of social stratification commonly know, in the critique of mainstream occupational mobility and status attainment research. His production of a so-called empirically based Marxist alternative to the mainstream stratification models made him well known and in demand.[13]

The publication of *Class, Crisis and the State,* especially its "Methodological Introduction," served as a kind of manifesto for a new generation of radical-leaning sociology graduate students trained in quantitative statistical methods and mainstream research techniques. Perhaps because of the greater respectability and "scientific" character of this "new" quantitative-oriented sociologized Marxism, Wright's inclination toward mathematics, natural science, and attitudinal survey research have been rewarded with academic notoriety and pay dirt.[14]

With the publication of *Class, Crisis and the State* extending an Althusserian/Poulantzian yet "empirical" approach to Marxism (this had been an alleged principal deficiency of his mentors), Wright rose to the bourgeois challenge to "prove" Marxist theory.[15] It now appeared possible to assert, with *social scientific* authority, the superiority of Marxism when practiced as a fusion of Althusserian/Poulantzian Marxism with mainstream empirical sociological methods.[16]

While there have been extended criticisms of Althusserian Marxism,[17] these have mostly concerned the specific fallacies of "structuralism" and have not been critiques of the very possibility of sociologized Marxism, nor of the broader "scientific theoretical" project of producing an "objective" (in the neo-Kantian and sociological sense) knowledge of "external," "objective" structures. The U.S.-based reception of Althusserian Nicos Poulantzas's work on class structure and capitalist state theory has been subjected to the same kinds of criticisms as those directed toward Althusserianism generally.[18]

Moreover, even the most prominent "post-Althusserian" influences on Wright's practice of Marxist method produce a reading of Marx's argument compatible with that of Althusser.[19] This is certainly no surprise, since they all buttress *academic* grounding practiced in its narrowest sense, whether as a neoclassical economics, social psychology, or analytical philosophy. Within Wright's "realist" Marxism, this especially applies to the twin facets of the "scientific" Marxist proponents' argument: (1) trivialization and marginalization of most of Marx's argument predating *Capital* (and even reading *Capital* itself as a variant of neoclassical "economic science"); and (2) a commitment to treating Marxism as a variant of bourgeois sociological theory.[20]

It is remarkable that Althusser's own criticisms of his previous work, especially his essay "Elements of Self Criticism" in *Essays in Self Criticism* (1976) have not been developed nor acknowledged in any fundamental way by Wright. This text, while retaining his basic commitment to Marxism as Marxist *science* (at least Althusser's particular appropriation of "science"), was very critical of a number of key assumptions made in his earlier work. In fact, his admissions that (1) the attempt to create a Marxist epistemology was seriously flawed; (2) his previous distinction between science and ideology was based on a "speculative-rationalist" fallacy; and (3) his theorization of scientific practice as "theoretical practice" had serious deficiencies could have been developed in many serious ways by Wright. We can only speculate that the specter of a defeated Leninist fusion of theory and practice (as Althusser practiced this separation of a "theorics" embodied in the party cadre-theoretician) prevented Althusser from going all the way and, perhaps, kept Wright from doing the same.

Obscured and mostly absent from the U.S.-based sociological criticisms of "structural Marxism" was the question whether there could be a sociologized Marxism — whether this was not in fact a contradictory practice. Althusserians may have been accused of too much determinism and structuralism, but the question whether sociologized Marxism as "scientific" theory was a legitimate practice was not at issue.[21]

While I have concerned myself with situating Wright's work, this is to imply a broader critique of what Marxism has become — at least in its academically sociologized practice. In his latest book, *Classes* (1985b) Wright declares that he is both a "Marxist materialist and class analyst" (p.3). My basic aim throughout this critique is to reveal the impossibility of such a claim, yet the necessity with which he must defend it.

Notes

1. See Marx and Engels (1975, 303) for Marx's specific critique of abstract materialism in natural science as a form of idealism. Marx's more general critique of contemplative abstract materialism can be found throughout Marx's texts, since it is precisely this production of materialism that is endemic to the abstract labor premise of liberalist social and political theory.

2. The necessity of fundamentally transforming what has become an ossified bourgeois practice of Marx's critique certainly did not begin in the 1980s but has its grounding in efforts over the last hundred years to "de-Kantianize" and "de-naturalize" what came to be the dominant Marxisms of the Second and Third Internationals. Unfortunately, rather than Wright's present-day "Marxist sociology" being part of the critical response to re-Kantianized Marxism, his entire project relies on its very pre-Marxist and bourgeois authority. Wright's practice of social science is in fact the

major non-Marxist direction that this post-Kantian science/philosophy/ practice has gone. Hypothetico-deductive claims grounded in the model of natural science, statistical inference grounded in mathematics, and a principle of agency grounded in liberalist social theory are not just a circumvention of Marx's critique of Hegel, but a totally different pre-Marxist bourgeois practice. The new "post-Comtean" social physicists have far more in common with Newton, Bacon, Locke, and the philosophers of "industrial capitalism" than Marx's revolution against not only capitalist social relations but its philosophical exponents as well. The frightening possiblity remains that these same sociologized Marxists will herald the necessity of "post-Marxism," on the grounds not of their real failure to practice Marxism but the alleged inability of Marxism to provide direction to revolutionizing practice! See Wright (1987) for the latest statement regarding Wright's excitement and interest in so-called post-Marxist radical social theory.

3. See Anderson (1976).

4. Marx's "early works" refers primarily to those works produced by Marx before *The German Ideology* (1845). It is important to note that several of these texts had been unavailable until the 1930s, and the English translations even later than that. The *Grundrisse* will also be considered central to a discussion of Marx's argument. Its appearance in 1941, almost a hundred years after its production, has served to demonstrate the crucial continuity between Marx's early arguments and *Capital,* as well as Marx's central project of a critique of alienated labor under capitalism. Given this continuity, *Capital* can be understood not as a doctrine comprised of scientific economic theorems and a new "Marxist" political economy but as a critique of alienated objectification under capitalist commodity production.

5. For two contemporary accounts that reveal the structure of such a comparative project, see "Marxism and Sociology" by Richard Flacks in Ollman and Vernoff (1982) and the "Introduction" and "Part I" of Bottomore and Goode (1983).

   See, Bottomore's essay, "Sociology" in McLellan (1983) for the following claims: Positivism is central to any Marxist theory, and Marxists "can defend their methodology, if necessary, with the help of other philosophies of science, such as the new realism, or some versions of neo-Kantianism (which may be related in various ways to realism)."

6. See "Introduction" to Althusser (1969) for an expression of this period in France.

7. See Thompson (1978) for his understanding of Althusserianism's impact on the "debates" within British Marxism in general but, most especially, on

the prospects for *New Left Review*. See also Anderson (1980) for a critique of Thompson (1978).

8. The development of what has come to be called "dialectical materialism" has its grounding over an extended period in Soviet Communist practice. The Russian philosopher and Second International luminary Plekhanov had already coined the term "materialist dialectic," practicing this term within the context of a non-Marxist Russian materialist tradition. But the specific production of a "dialectical materialism" stems from the Soviet attempts to build a coherent, universalizable naturalist dialectic from Engels's extant manuscripts/notebooks posthumously entitled *The Dialectics of Nature*. These notebooks, combined with Engels's *Anti-Duhring* and Lenin's philosophical grounding in a reflection theory of knowledge (i.e., *Materialism and Empirio-Criticism)* became the basis for a revitalization of what amounted to a naturalistically conceived epistemology, in fact, a throwback to pre-Marxist views. Bukharin's argument explicitly reinforced Soviet DIAMAT by arguing the necessary separation of a philosophy from a naturalistically conceived sociology. In light of the consolidiation of Soviet DIAMAT from Plekhanov to Bukharin, Althusser's contributions are anything but unique. Of course, the common denominator for all is the necessity they attribute to the radical separation of party cadre-theoreticians from other merely historical workers. Far from being based in Marx's practice of the labor process, however, Soviet DIAMAT is a retrograde yet contemporary effort at resuscitating the traditional privilege accorded to philosophy.

   Though there are basic problems with Antonio Gramsci's re-Hegelianized and Leninized practice of Marxism, his criticisms of the relation between Soviet DIAMAT and pre-Marxist materialism provide a very useful counterpoint to Wright's sociologized Marxism. See Gramsci's critique of Bukharin's *Theory of Historical Materialism: A Popular Manual of Marxist Sociology* in Gramsci (1971, 419-472).

9. Althusser (1976, 114-115), where Althusser claims that "the 'left' critique of the idea of a Marxist science can already be found in the young Lukacs, Korsch, Pannekoek, etc.?"

10. This claim is widely cited in several works. For two examples, see Burawoy (1982, S6) and McLellan (1979, 299-306).

11. For instance, many of the essays appearing in English in *For Marx* (1969) and *Reading Capital* (1970) had been written and debated between 1960 and 1965 in French Communist party circles.

12. In the case of Wright, see "Marxist Class Categories and Income Inequality" (1977) and "Race, Class and Income Inequality" (1978a). For the claim that

New Left Review, Insurgent Sociologist and *Kapitalistate* were major outlets for Althusserianism, see Burawoy (1982, S6).

It is noteworthy that Wright's earliest publications appeared in these journals. See "Modes of Class Struggle and the Capitalist State" Wright et al. (1976); "Class Boundaries in Advanced Capitalist Society" (1976); "Intellectuals and the Working Class" (1978b). These publications coincided with editorial and governing positions on two of these journals — member of editorial board of *Kapitalistate* (1973-76) and member of the board of directors of *Insurgent Sociologist* (1976-78).

13. See the Social Science Citation Index for an example of widespread citation of Wright's work in the mid to late 1970s, especially, *Class, Crisis and the State.*

14. Wright's inclination toward mathematics and the model of positivist natural science may be evidenced by the following accolades and publications (sources from *Curriculum Vitae,* September 1985): (1963) received 4th place in biological science at National Science Fair-International; (1964) received 1st place in mathematics at National Science Fair-International. See also Wright's first three journal articles: "Response to Auditory Stimulus in the Developing Rat" (1963), "Analysis of the Total Number of Twists Resulting from Cutting Any Order Moebius Band With Any Number of Cuts" (1964) and "A Study of Student Leaves of Absence" (1973).

It is interesting that Wright's parents were both psychology professors at the University of Kansas at the time of his publications.

For an indication of the notoriety and pay dirt, see the "Preface" to Wright (1985b) where Wright indicates that he has "also become integrated into a nexus of rewards that is very alluring." He goes on to say that "my research on class has led to a series of large research grants which pay parts of my salary and allow me to take time off from teaching to write. As my reputation has grown, I have had numerous opportunities for travel and lecturing in various places around the world. And I have been handsomely rewarded by my Sociology Department and University of Wisconsin."

15. See "Methodological Introduction" (1979a, 9) for the challenge, and the following pages for his construction of a response to this challenge.

16. Wright (1979a, 10-14). Burawoy (1982, S28), on the other hand, while relying on Gouldner, constructs a different understanding of the relationship between Marxism and sociology. The significance of his defense of Marxism and academic sociology as scientific theory should be focalized here. "In the final analysis, Marxism can never become anything more than a subordinate presence within the university if it is to retain its oppositional character. But that presence may not only push Marxism in new directions

but may also be necessary for the vitality of sociology." He continues, ". . . the renewal of an open, always provisional, empirically rooted Marxism could do much to animate debate over those issues at the heart of the Sociological tradition. As Alvin Gouldner once wrote, Marxism and Sociology are like Siamese twins, 'The demise of one presages the demise of the other. They have a common destiny not despite the fact that they have developed in dialectical opposition but precisely because of it.'"

17. For examples of criticisms of "structuralist Marxism," see Norman Geras (1972), Glucksman (1972), Vilar (1973), Callinicos (1976), Thompson (1978), McLellan (1979, 303), Anderson (1980), Schmidt (1981), Benton (1984). See Wood (1986) for an excellent critique not only of Althusser but of the "retreat from class" at the heart of Althusser and his most important followers and the strategic/political implications of this retreat.

18. This claim is important, since Poulantzas argued within a highly scientized Althusserianism. See, for example, his extensive reliance and use of *Reading Capital* and *For Marx* in his early work, especially the "Introduction" to Poulantzas (1973).

19. Keat and Urry (1982); John Roemer (1981 and 1982a). These works are selected for basically three reasons. First, Wright himself explicitly acknowledges his indebtedness to Roemer and the "analytical Marxism" of persons working within the same premises; see Preface to *Classes*. Second, Wright's 1983-84 syllabus for his one-year course on "The Theory and Methodology of Marxist Social Science" (SOC 621, 622), especially the section "Epistemological and Methodological Problems," relies heavily on the work of Keat and Urry. The realist reading of Marx informs Wright's entire treatment of science and so-called concept formation. For example, consider Wright's claim that Marxist method, once cleansed of Hegel, is very much like other methods of science. In a footnote to Wright (1983a), he asserts what characterizes a Marxist method from bourgeois method. The distinctiveness of Marxism, he argues, does not lie in its method "because when 'Marxist method' is properly specified and its tendencies towards Hegelianism eliminated, then in general its prescriptions are no longer unique to Marxism." Wright's "realist" reading of Marx's argument here reduces Marxism to some version of positivist social theory rooted in the classical model of natural and social science. Finally, Wright's use of Roemer's argument indicates a reliance on Roemer's analytical "realism" for his own argument in *Classes*.

20. For the relationship between the repression of Marx's early arguments and the possibility of an objective realist science, See Keat and Urry (1982, 6,116-117,264). For a defense of Marxism as scientific theory and the role of mathematical modeling for producing an "objective standard for

deciding which is correct," see Roemer (1981, 2,3,7). See also Roemer (1982a, 23-24) for a reading of Marxism as a historical materialism reducible to economic structure.

21. As pointed out previously, at least one Marxist sociologist, Tom Bottomore, revels in this triumph of scientific Marxist sociology.

Chapter 2   "Methodological Individualism" and the Specter of The Masochistic Proletariat

Any argument concerning class structure presupposes a determinant practice of subjectivity. One might have expected Wright to argue this principle of subjectivity much earlier in his text, but as it turns out, his first explicit and extensive elaboration is to be found in chapter 7 of *Classes*. Entitled "Class Consciousness and Class Structure in Contemporary Capitalism," this chapter accordingly provides the point of departure for my critique of Wright's class structure argument. The basic claim I argue is that Wright's principle of subjectivity prohibits him from producing a true and objective knowledge of class structure. In other words, if we accept Wright's construction of consciousness and class consciousness on their own terms, it is not possible to ground a knowledge of the class structure. Since Marxism should be concerned to establish a firm grounding for class analysis in a determinant practice of the labor process, Wright's "methodological individualism" and "rational actor" theory must provide such a point of departure.

I also argue several subsidiary claims. First, in order to achieve the central goal of his chapter 7, Wright dispenses with a Marxist practice of class consciousness and substitutes mainstream sociological attitudinal survey research in its place. The production of the social-psychological dependent variable "class attitude" is central to his goal, since it can function to verify Wright's "new" class map, whereas practices of class consciousness that endanger this objective are not developed.

29

Second, Wright's recent theorization of subjectivity is a response to the crisis of the Althusserian-based functional-*Trager* subject that had permeated much of Wright's work until *Classes*. This new intentionalist "rational actor," based squarely within the traditions of bourgeois neoclassical economics, social psychology, and analytic philosophy, replaces Wright's mere functional bearer of social relations as the new agent of social structure. Several objections can be raised against this latest and apparently novel attempt to revive liberalism as ground for a principle of agency.

Third, Wright posits an extremely non-Marxist and contradictory theory of "objective interests." Contrary to Marxist practices, which ground objectivity within the capitalist labor process, Wright's interests are alleged to be universal in a Kantian-essentialist sense and at the same time to be possible objects of scientific knowledge. Wright's many attempts to authorize the objectivity of these interests get tangled in hopeless contradictions. I argue that the maintenance of a fact-value distinction provides the basis for Wright's theory of "objective interests" and that this same distinction leads to the specter of the masochistic proletariat.

Finally, I conclude by asserting the necessity with which Wright must attempt to overcome epistemological relativism through reliance on a special theory of the labor process, one that is allegedly immune from conditions that give rise to the relativist predicament. Sociologized Marxism is Wright's response to the inescapable subjectivism engulfing Wright's nonscientific "rational actor."

Wright initiates his discussion of consciousness with reference to a debate over the epistemological status of consciousness in Marxist theory. On one hand, he claims, "'Structuralist' writers in the tradition of Louis Althusser have argued that consciousness is an epistemologically suspect category and of dubious explanatory relevance," whereas "Marxists identified with the 'humanist marxist' tradition have placed con-

sciousness at the center of their analysis" (Wright 1985b, 241).
With this dual schema as premise, he asserts,

> One of the hallmarks of these Marxist debates over
> consciousness is the tendency to be preoccupied with
> philosophical and methodological issues. The idiom
> of the discussion revolves around questions of
> whether or not human beings are the "authors" of
> their own acts, whether intentions have explanatory
> power, whether the distinction between "subjects"
> and "objects" is an admissable one, and so on. The
> result is that, with relatively rare exceptions, the
> systematic discussion of class consciousness in the
> Marxist tradition has not focused on empirical prob-
> lems of its explanation and consequences. (Ibid.)

In terms of these alleged deficiencies in the Marxist discussions
of class consciousness, Wright then lays out his chapter's objective.

> The central purpose of this chapter is to examine the
> empirical relation between class structure and an at-
> titudinal measure of class consciousness. (Ibid.)

Not only are there two basic Marxist approaches to consciousness as an epistemological category, there "are two quite
different usages of the expression 'class consciousness' in the
Marxist tradition." Some theorists claim that class consciousness is "a counterfactual or imputed characteristic of
classes as collective entities" while others argue that it should be
"understood as a concrete attribute of human individuals as
members of classes" (ibid., 242). Singling out Georg Lukacs as a
probable best representative of the former usage of class consciousness, Wright then goes on to criticize him. Lukacs is not
faulted for the "humanist marxist" fallacy of placing con-

sciousness at the center of analysis but for practicing consciousness at a supraindividual level.

For instance, consider the following excerpt from Lukacs's
History and Class Consciousness (1971), which Wright uses to
construct a criticism of Lukacs's argument.

> Now class consciousness consists in fact of the ap-
> propriate and rational reactions imputed to a par-
> ticular position in the process of production. This
> consciousness is, therefore, neither the sum nor the
> average of what is thought or felt by the single in-
> dividuals who make up the class. And yet the histor-
> ically significant actions of the class as a whole are
> determined in the last resort by this consciousness
> and not by the thought of the individual — and these
> actions can be understood only by reference to this
> consciousness. (P. 51.)

While there are important criticisms of Lukacs's objective
idealism in the Marxist literature, including the later (1967)
Lukacs himself, Wright's criticism is based on a different concern. Wright is not objecting to a practice of objective idealism — a
condition where objective truth-meaning preexist in the social
structure and the proletarian class, by virtue of its incumbency
in this structure, is "imputed" with the "objective meaning" or
"consciousness" of its historic mission. Lukacs explicitly admitted that the basis for such a formulation was his fundamentally
mistaken conflation of objectification with alienation. Rather,
Wright critiques Lukacs for implying that "class consciousness
as a causally efficacious mechanism . . . is an attribute of classes
as such, not of the individuals who make up that class." Consequently, what is important for determining historical trajectories "is this consciousness of the class *per se*" (Wright 1985,
243).

Wright argues that "it is this insistence on the causal power of supra-individual consciousness that makes Lukacs' work vulnerable to the critique that it is fundamentally committed to an objective teleology of history" (ibid.) Wright adopts this critique of "objective teleology" from Jon Elster, most probably Elster's 1982 *Theory and Society* article extensively cited in *Classes*. Elster defines objective teleology as those "processes guided by a purpose without an intentional subject" and, in contradistinction, defines subjective teleology as "intentional acts with an intentional subject" (Elster 1982, 454-455).

In short, Wright is rejecting Lukacs's argument on the grounds that he does not posit an *intentional individual subject* as the producer and bearer of class consciousness. Thus, absence of an intentionalist subjectivity, not a re-Hegelianized objective idealism, is the thrust of Wright's claim against an "objective teleology of history."

After rejecting Lukacs in these terms, Wright offers his approach to class consciousness. According to Wright, the "second general usage of the expression 'class consciousness' identifies it as a particular aspect of the concrete subjectivity of individuals" (Wright 1985b, 243). The most distinctive characteristic of this approach is its claim to define consciousness as a property of unique and separate individuals rather than at the level of "supra-individual" processes and/or structures. Wright reasons: "Such supra-individual entities, and in particular 'classes,' do not have consciousness in the literal sense since they are not the kind of entities which have minds, which think, weigh alternatives, have preferences, etc" (ibid.).

Wright is aware of other approaches to class consciousness, yet insists on authorizing consciousness as proper to the subjectivity of an intentionalist "rational actor." In a remarkable footnote, he offers a glimpse of this alternative, claiming:

There is one sense in which one could legitimately refer to "class consciousness" as a property of a collectivity, namely when consciousness is used to describe the practices themselves and not simply the forms of subjectivity that shape the intentional choices implicated in those practices. Since the actual practices involve the use of organizational resources and various other kinds of collective capacities, *when the term "consciousness" is extended to cover the practices as such, then it is no longer strictly an attribute of individuals* (Ibid., 280; italics added.)

Wright's legitimation of this alternative approach to "consciousness" directly challenges his effort to construct "class consciousness" as a property of individualized attitudinal states. If, as Wright here suggests, consciousness is practiced as the indivisible unity of class practices, then how would Wright propose to achieve his central chapter objective, namely, to "examine the empirical relation between class structure and an attitudinal measure of class consciousness"?

There can exist, by Wright's explicit admission, a legitimate practice of consciousness that cannot be practiced in terms of an individually incarcerated attitudinal state. Because of his reliance on the dependent variable "class attitude" for "empirical verification" of his claims on class structure, however, Wright must deny this indivisible unity of class practices. In short, if a social-psychologized dependent variable is to be constructed, then all arguments denying the intentionalist grounding for class consciousness must be dismissed. This provides a clear example of sociologism necessarily avoiding Marxism on the crucial questions concerning a principle of subjectivity and agency. And since subjectivity and agency are in actuality produced within a determinate labor process, this marks a fundamental departure from Marxism on the question of the meaning and significance of the capitalist labor process itself.

Retreating without explanation, Wright backs down from this legitimate alternative approach. Proceeding as if no dilemma has been created, Wright concludes:

> I prefer to limit the expression consciousness to the subjective dimensions of the problem, and use the term capacities to describe the collectively organized resources used in struggles, and the term practices to describe the individual and collective activities that result from the linkage of individual consciousness and collective capacities. (Ibid.)

The above claim is unwarranted given that Wright clearly indicates the possibility of at least two legitimate practices of subjectivity. One usage includes capacities and practices as its definition, whereas the second approach circumscribes consciousness to a "particular aspect of the concrete subjectivity of individuals." Both are offered as legitimate practices of the "subjective dimensions of the problem," and Wright offers no explicit rationale for his preference to develop a practice of the capitalist labor process in terms of the minimalist confines of individual mental life.

The unwarranted manner in which Wright dismisses a legitimate alternative gives more credence to the notion that non-Marxist considerations are governing the production of Wright's discussion of class consciousness. While I have indicated Wright's subsumption of Marxism to his declared chapter objective of producing the "dependent variable" this is not the entire story. There is a broader and perhaps much more strategically important consideration governing Wright's practice of subjectivity and class consciousness.

I shall argue that Wright's employment of Jon Elster, in particular, is a response to the "problem of agency" in Wright's argument, as it has been and remains so for many Althusserians. This response is at the heart of Wright's recent theorization of subjectivity and should serve as a premise for the production of my specific critique of Wright's construction of class consciousness.[1]

The general presupposition of subjectivity that Wright deploys in *Classes* comes from the work of Jon Elster. Wright, citing Elster (1982), indicates this in an endnote to chapter 7.

> The abstract conceptualization of consciousness and class consciousness adopted in this chapter is rooted in a view of human action that is sometimes referred to as "rational choice" or "strategic action theory." (Wright 1985b, 280-281.)

Corresponding to this general presupposition of abstract egoistic individualism is a doctrine self-described as "methodological individualism." According to two of its proponents, Jon Elster and John Roemer, this doctrine can provide a basis for understanding the hitherto mysterious and unexplained "microfoundations" of macrostructures. According to Elster (1982),

> By methodological individualism I mean the doctrine that all social phenomena (their structure and their change) are in principle explicable only in terms of individuals — their properties, goals and beliefs. (P. 453.)

Furthermore, according to Elster, "insistence on methodological individualism leads to a search for microfoundations of Marxist social theory," and these microfoundations are best grounded in "social psychology" (ibid., 454).

In the same issue of *Theory and Society* in which Elster's 1982 article appeared, John Roemer, another central influence on Wright's latest theorization of class structure, produces a defense of Elster's position. Speaking specifically to the issue of class analysis in his essay "Methodological Individualism and

Deductive Marxism," Roemer (1982b) insists that "class analysis must have individualist foundations" (p. 513). And where do these foundations come from? The "basic postulates on individual behavior" can be stated, since they "are sufficiently fundamental to be considered self-evident" (ibid., 514)—although in the next breath he claims that these "postulates may be proposed . . . on the basis of prior inductive evidence" (ibid.).

While it is accurate to say that Elster's critique is grounded in an analytical philosophical critique of functionalist explanation in social theory, Roemer's critique is not. Roemer's reasons for rejecting the capitalist labor process as a ground for class analysis stems from his basic rejection of the labor theory of value. While Marxists may be divided on the precise meaning of the labor theory of value, Roemer seems to reject the capitalist labor process altogether as a realm of historical determination. Instead of class being produced within and through the process of self-objectification occuring within relations of capitalist control over the labor process and means of production, Roemer "deduces" class "endogenously" from a premise of unequal exchange between two unequally endowed economic agents.

> It is noteworthy that class position is determined *endogenously* in the model, as a consequence of individual optimization in the face of a constraint determined by one's ownership of productive assets. (Roemer 1982a, 15.)

Furthermore, given what Roemer terms his "game-theoretic definition in which property relations, not the labor theory of value, is the central concept" (ibid., 19-20), rather than begin with the direct relation of the worker in production, Roemer (ibid.) begins with the "self-evident" individuals of bourgeois liberalist neoclassical theory: "But an important conclusion . . . is that it is the differential ownership of productive assets, rather than what happens in the labor process, that is the key determinant of Marxian exploitation" (p. 16).

I argue that the significance of this movement to bring the bourgeois liberalist "rational actor" back lies, not in the particular alternative it presents, but in its relation to both bourgeois social science and Althusserian and so-called post-Althusserian Marxism. In short, "methodological individualism" is Wright's and others'[2] response to the "problem of agency" confronting what amounted to Althusserian Marxian structural functionalism.

The label "structural functionalism"—usually associated with mainstream Parsonianism in sociology—is actually apropos for describing Althusserianism, since the subject-as-agent-of-history is reduced to a mere bearer, or *Trager,* of the structure. *The subject functions to reproduce the structure and history is the product of successive functional reproductions of structures.* Within an Althusserian practice of subjectivity, there is virtually no role for "the subject" beyond that necessitated by "the structure." But what guarantees this? What ensures this reproduction of structures?

For Wright and many other sociologized Althusserians, functional explanation in social theory guaranteed the functional reproduction of dominating structures.[3] The critique of functional explanation has successfully problematized the question of historical reproduction and has created a space for alternative practices of subjectivity. And, most significantly, the sociologized Althusserian "reading out" of Marx's early arguments regarding labor, alienated labor, and a class' conscious being created the basis for moving away from Marxism on these most crucial questions. Or, in the case of Elster, reading Marx as a "pioneer" in game theory has turned Marx's argument into a variant of bourgeois liberalism. "Methodological Individualism" and "rational-choice theory" are alleged to do what functional explanation (and by implication, Marxism itself) cannot—namely, provide a coherent rationale in defense of the contingent, historicality with which the "social structure" is actually reproduced.[4]

The real key to social structure, according to methodological individualism, is to be found not in the objective activity of labor but in the abstract labor premises of economics, cognitive psychology, and moral philosophy.[5] Although from the standpoint of a critique of tautological functionalism, this may appear to advance discussions of human agency, this has very little in common with my reading of Marx's argument on class consciousness. The "self-evident" individual Roemer speaks of is no more than the abstract individual of classical materialism. As Marx (Marx and Engels 1976) remarks, "The highest point attained by *contemplative* materialism, that is, materialism which does not comprehend sensuousness as practical activity, is the contemplation of single individuals in 'civil society'" (p. 8).

Wright's argument in *Classes* is part of the strategic response to the "problem of agency" confronting practitioners of bourgeois social science as well as his own Althusserian Marxism. The considerable significance this holds for shaping Wright's latest argument on class consciousness should not be underestimated, and a more extended examination of this movement is certainly warranted. A thoroughgoing critique of this entire movement would certainly augment an understanding of Wright's project, but I now return to Wright's specific argument in *Classes*.

According to Wright, "Understood in this way," to study "consciousness" is "to study a particular aspect of the mental life of individuals, namely, those elements of a persons subjectivity which are *discursively accessible to the individuals own awareness*" (Wright 1985b, 244).

There are several crucial distinctions with respect to the domain of this "consciousness." The first distinction, according to Wright, is the one separating consciousness from unconsciousness. Discursive accessibility to the individual's own awareness, as noted above, defines consciousness, whereas the unconscious is defined as "the discursively inaccessible aspects of mental life" (ibid.). Constitutive of this conscious domain we have what Wright terms the "elements of consciousness." "The elements of consciousness," according to Wright, include "beliefs, ideas, observations, information, theories, preferences" (ibid.).

How does this division of consciousness into conscious-unconscious realms affect Wright's effort to attain an objective knowledge of class structure? On the one hand, Wright claims that "from the point of view of social theory the most important way in which consciousness figures in social explanations is in the way it is implicated in the intentions and resulting choices of actors" (ibid.). Although Wright argues that this "is not to suggest, of course, that *subjectivity* only has effects through intentional choices; a wide range of psychological mechanisms may directly influence behavior without passing through conscious intention" (ibid.).

Moreover, not only can nonintentional psychological mechanisms operate decisively to influence behavior, nonintentional macrostructures can effect social outcomes as well.

> It may well be that the crucial determinants are to be found in the processes which determine the range of possible courses of action open to actors, rather than in the actual conscious processes implicated in the choice among those alternatives. (Ibid., 244-245.)

Despite postulating the operation of unconscious psychological and structural processes as crucial determinants of individual rationality and choice (including knowledges), Wright focuses on intentional choice by invoking "the point of view of social theory." Since social theory (as Wright constructs this practice) claims that individualist-based *conscious, intentional rationality and choice* is a necessary ground for studying social structures, it follows that studying conscious intentionality rather than these basic social-structural and psychostructural foundations is clearly warranted. Wright concludes, in apparent disregard of the magnitude of the questions raised by this fundamental dichotomy, that

> in order to understand fully the real mechanisms that link social structures to social practices, the subjective basis of the intentional choices made by the actors who live within those structures and engage in those practices must be investigated, and this implies studying consciousness. (Ibid., 245.)

Wright's argument on class consciousness presents several difficulties for producing an objective and reliable knowledge of class structure. First, Wright has admitted that unconscious, unintentional psychological mechanisms may be just as important for constituting social practices as conscious intentional ones. If, by definition, they are "discursively inaccessible," then how is this unintentional psychological domain to be studied?

Second, earlier in his argument Wright claims that his "conceptualization of consciousness is closely bound up with the problem of *will* and *intentionality.*" Wright claims that to "say something is subjectively accessible is to say that by an act of will the person can make themselves aware of it" (ibid., 244). Wright's introduction of this metaphysical category "will" for attaining any awareness of "dormant" elements of consciousness (e.g., information, observation, preferences) remains unexplained. If subjective accessibility is a function of awareness, and awareness is a function of "will," of what is "will" a function? What are the conditions for the production of "will"? Wright is conspicuously silent on this point. Are we to assume that "will" is that classic category of Kantian and pre-Marxist philosophy alleged to overcome the specter of determinism in a schema of natural causality, and similar to the categories "mind," "soul," and "conception" that distinguish us from mere brute animals? This grounding of freedom (and knowledge) in a principle of intelligibility that resides outside nature (and by implication, outside history) is most certainly at the heart of Kantian ethics and science, something Wright is either unaware of or considers compatible with a Marxist practice.

Perhaps this is just another feature of Wright's liberalist "rational choice" individualism — in this case, the agent is characterized by some mysterious willful energizing principle responsible itself for producing human consciousness and rationality. In any case, it is nowhere to be discovered; rather it is posited as if self-evident.

Finally, even if the psychological black box is correctly tuned, and if "will" really does make the stuff of consciousness discursively accessible, Wright still faces a major obstacle. Recall that he claimed that the necessary "crucial determinants [of consciousness] are to be found in the processes which determine the range of possible choice . . . rather than in the actual conscious processes implicated in the choice among those alternatives." There is no indication of how Wright, given a consciousness constructed within the terms of a merely conscious intentionality, can ever arrive at a knowledge of these determinants, and by implication, achieve a basis for grounding knowledge of class structure.

The second major demarcation of consciousness Wright argues is an alleged distinction between "Culture" and "Ideology." These domains are characterized by their respective "effects" embedded in consciousness. "Culture," according to Wright, consists of "social practices, or perhaps more precisely, that dimension of social practice, which shapes the non-conscious aspects of subjectivity: character structure, personality, habits, affective styles, etc." (ibid., 245).

In contradistinction to Culture, Wright says Ideology concerns "the process of the formation of human *consciousness*" (ibid.) In a footnote, Wright claims:

> Ideology and Culture are not two distinct kinds of
> events in the world. In the actual practices of social

actors they are continually intertwined. The distinction being made is between the kinds of effects produced by given practices. Ideological effects are effects centered on consciousness and cognition; cultural effects are effects centered on non-conscious aspects of subjectivity. (Ibid., 281.)

Having established the practical significance of unconscious psychological and social processes (and by implication, knowledges of these practices), Wright makes a similar claim for Culture. As an example of the Culture-Ideology distinction, he writes that whereas "ideology produces beliefs in both the desirability of competition as a way of life and the inevitability of aggressive competitiveness as a mode of human interaction: culture, on the other hand, produces the competitive personalities capable of acting on those beliefs in an effective manner" (ibid., 245).

This extraordinarily murky part of Wright's argument on class consciousness seems to ground itself in a *Trager,* or subject-as-bearer-of properties. In his schema, some properties are "cultural" (character, habits, etc.) and some are "ideological." The "ideological" (beliefs, knowledges, ideas, etc.) properties are of "consciousness" and are, at least in part, representational (thus, his individual can have beliefs *about,* ideas *of,* etc., his/her character, habits, etc., but those beliefs or ideas are *not* the same as the character, habits, etc.) It appears that the "ideological" properties are in some sense housed in and energized by the "cultural" properties. Analogous to the role of the unconscious in Wright's already bifurcated subjectivity, meaning itself is constituted through and energized by a structure internal to the psyche. In Wright's argument, cultural practices (as distinct from ideological ones) have their effects on consciousness by creating structures shaping the variety of choices available to Wright's "rational actor."

Culture itself is expressed through the unconscious dimensions of the psyche (e.g., the "personality structure") and, according to Wright, may provide the key to this enigmatic process of knowledge production.

> It may well be the case that culture is considerably more important than ideology: beliefs in competitiveness may be reproducible in a society only so long as they conform to appropriate personality structures. (Ibid.)

Mimicking his previous claim vis-á-vis the primacy of nonintentional processes, Wright asserts that "this would correspond to the claim that the conscious dimensions of human subjectivity matter much less than the unconscious ones in explaining social practices" (ibid.).

At the least, based on the above claims, we can conclude that Wright's mysterious "rational actor" presents formidable obstacles for attempted attitudinal empirical quantification. Earlier, Wright claimed that for beliefs, observations, theories, etc., to be discursively accessible to an individual's own awareness, an act of will must be forthcoming. In its own terms, however, this inaccessible "will" defies examination. It functions, rather, as it did for Kant, as an ahistorical-anatural principle located in a faculty of intelligibility (pure reason) grounding the possibility of freedom (and knowledge) rather than in any Marxist practice of consciousness. Even if we accept the validity of Wright's definition of consciousness (with its accompanying reliance on "will"), Wright is still in a lurch, since by his own admission "the unconscious dimensions of the psyche" are more important for explaining social practice.

With respect to these "unconscious dimensions," several problems previously alluded to need to be resolved. If they are "unconscious" processes, how is Wright himself capable of "consciously" and "intentionally" having knowledge of them?

By definition, this is the realm of the *un*thinkable. Second, even if Wright allows himself the liberty of rational activity, the unconscious realm of the psyche exists in a state of discursive inaccessibility. It is the other side of consciousness complementing conscious subjectivity and intentional choice. By virtue of this discursive inaccessibility (*read:* inaccessibility to *reason*) Wright can never be sure that observations, theorizations, etc., are controlled by him and subject to his intentions. This "black box" cannot be rationally comprehended, since it provides the unconscious structural conditions constituting rationality itself.

Wright faces an insuperable contradiction. On the one hand, rationality is a necessary presupposition for generating a knowledge of the conditions of this "class structure." On the other hand, rationality cannot be presupposed, since Wright cannot presuppose what he must prove, namely, how and in what ways rationality is determined by these nonintentional structures. The existence of nonintentional and unconscious processes cannot be proven in the terms of Wright's argument, they can only be articles of faith for a given *intentional* actor. Furthermore, and despite the fundamental role these nonintentional structures have in determining consciousness, Wright still claims social theory should be more concerned with how consciousness "is implicated in the intentions and resulting choices of actors." This does not follow, especially since Wright has failed to articulate the conditions producing both unconscious and conscious subjectivity. It of course does follow if Wright's primary concern is adherence to the premise of bourgeois liberalist "rational actor" theory.

Unyielding in his effort to authorize the "rational actor's" *conscious* intentionality as the legitimate concern of social theory, Wright produces a similarly unfounded conclusion regarding the culture-ideology distinction. Wright admits it "may well be the case that culture is considerably more important than ideology," but remarkably proceeds to conclude the following:

Nevertheless, our preoccupation in this chapter will be on consciousness, and for that reason, indirectly, on ideology. This implies that intentional action involving the conscious weighing of alternatives is an important property of social practice, and that its relationship to class is an important problem of social analysis. (Ibid., 245-246.)

Wright launches into a consideration of "ideology effects," despite the necessary and explicitly stated significance "culture effects" hold for constituting social practice. This is directly contradictory to his previous argument and provides further support for my earlier claim that Wright's construction of "consciousness" is designed to achieve his chapter's objective even at the expense of argumentative consistency, let alone a Marxist practice of class consciousness.

It appears Wright is willing to forsake a Marxist practice of consciousness for a social-psychological one. As an example of Wright's social psychologism, consider his attempt to demonstrate how "class structure" determines consciousness. Admitting this characterization "does not provide an account of precisely how class structure imposes these limits" (ibid., 29), Wright claims that, to discover how class consciousness is limited, we must conduct

an analysis of cognitive structures and social psychology, basically an analysis of the psychological process by which people come to understand the social determination of their capacities and options. (Ibid.)

Wright continues:

My assumption is that, however these psychological mechanisms operate, the real social mechanisms

operating in the world which shape the objective
capacities available to people impose the basic limits
on how people will view those capacities. (Ibid.)

Given his dilemma-ridden, contradictory previous argument,
Wright cannot begin to argue, let alone arrive at a knowledge of
class structure. In fact, his argument amounts to nothing less
than a traditional psychologistic causal theory of perception, a
view that Marx totally destroyed along with his critique of all
abstract-labor-based practices of knowledge production. Wright's
early training in psychology and natural science has been im-
ported for the purpose of shoring up and animating this otherwise empty, abstract "rational actor."

Since the conditions of conscious intentionality are necessarily
subject to unconscious psychological and cultural mechanisms —
mechanisms Wright has failed to elaborate — the process of
observation, theorization, preference formation remains mired
in obscurity. Subject to these mysterious unconscious and
unintended processes that shape all possible knowledges — including any knowledge of class structure — it is unclear how
Wright will even construct claims concerning the boundaries of
the class structure. If Wright should offer such claims, what
criteria will be brought to bear on them? Since unconscious processes, according to Wright, are more important than conscious
ones for constituting social practice, discriminations among
rival practices (e.g., truth claims) concerning the boundaries of
the "real" class structure are themselves in jeopardy.

Wright does not confront these implications of his construction of "consciousness" in general; instead, he proceeds to
specify properties of a "class consciousness" in identical terms.
Having circumscribed the domain of subjectivity without warrant,
this class consciousness will be constructed in terms of Wright's
"rational actor." Mainstream sociology's practice of "legitimate
science," not Marxism, allows such an unwarranted reduction

of a class' conscious being to terms of the dependent variable "class attitude."

According to Wright, "Class consciousness can be viewed as those aspects of consciousness with a distinctive class content to them" (ibid., 246). "Content" can mean one of two things.

> First, it can refer to a logical derivation of aspects of consciousness from an analysis of class. Alternatively, the class content of consciousness can refer to those aspects of consciousness which are implicated in intentions, choices and practices which have "class pertinent effects" in the world, effects on how individuals operate within a given structure of relations and effects on those relations themselves. (Ibid.)

Disregarding his previous argument specifying this domain (e.g., conscious intentionality) of subjectivity less crucial for explaining social practice, Wright nevertheless deploys the second approach to class consciousness. Wright begins to encounter serious difficulties, however, when trying to exactly define what "class content" means. To this point, "class content" has simply been defined in terms of "class pertinent effects." To avoid the charge that he is merely begging the question, Wright must now define what these "class pertinent effects" are.

Wright defines them in the most general terms as "effects on how individuals operate within a given structure of class relations and effects on those relations themselves." Consciousness directed at relations themselves affects one's "fundamental interests," whereas consciousness directed within relations affects one's "immediate interests."

Wright then proceeds to define "class pertinent effects" in terms of a definition of "class interests." This is necessary, since his definition of "class content" must implicitly rely on a notion of *class* interests defined in opposition to other theoretically subordinate interests. There are two different approaches to the relation between class consciousness and class interests. In the first, class consciousness

> constitutes a particular type of class-pertinent con-
> sciousness, namely a class-pertinent consciousness
> in which individuals have a relatively "true" and
> "consistent" understanding of their class interests.
> (Ibid.)

If Wright were to use this as his defining criterion for class consciousness, then he would have positively to assert what these "true" interests really are. Though Wright insists that a class structure is a "terrain of social relations that determine objective material interests of actors" (ibid.), he refuses to require a class knowledge of such interests as a criterion for class consciousness. One possible reason for this, I later argue, stems from Wright's failure to define what these interests really are. Second, if Wright were to define class-pertinent consciousness in terms of "true" interests (as he constructs "the true"), the pool of eligible sample respondents would be minuscule.

Wright, therefore, retreats and claims,

> I am using consciousness in a more general way to
> designate all forms of class pertinent consciousness
> *regardless of its faithfulness to real interests.* When I
> want to indicate specifically the presence of a par-
> ticular type of class consciousness, therefore, it will
> be necessary to employ suitable adjectives: pro-
> working class consciousness, anti-capitalist class
> consciousness, revolutionary working class con-
> sciousness, and so forth. (Ibid.; italics added.)

Wright eventually constructs an attitude scale in terms of two such "contents" — "pro-working class" and "anti-capitalist class" consciousness — and then uses this scale as a means of allegedly inferring from the effects of class structure (class attitude) the cause of these attitudes (Wright's concept of class structure).

Wright's construction of class consciousness, however, fails to demonstrate what "class pertinent consciousness" really is. His earlier ruling out of practice as constitutive of consciousness has led him instead to define consciousness as "the subjective processes that shape intentional choices." But if practice (class struggle, class formation, class organization, etc.) cannot be used to make discriminations concerning whether workers are class conscious or not, then how will a class' conscious being be determined or "measured"? Similarly, since Wright has ruled out "true" versus "false" interests as a means for making discriminations and in their place has constructed an attitude scale that measures how "pro-working class" or "anti-capitalist class" an individual is, how will Wright make *these* discriminations — "pro" and "anti"? According to Wright, even though "true" interests cannot be measured, he is allegedly able to measure different types of interests irrespective of "true" interests.

How does he arrive at a quality (quantity) called "pro-working class"? Does not this necessarily presuppose an objective standard for determining what constitutes *the* working-class interest? How can Wright even arrive at degrees of variance unless he posits an objective standard from which these may be said to vary, either "pro" or "anti"? If we take Wright at his word, the absence of a knowledge of "true" interests would make his discriminations "pro" and "anti" meaningless. So while Wright pays lip service to his claims opposing reliance on a notion of "true" interests, he in fact must presuppose them. In order to quantify "anti" and "pro" working-class attitudinal responses, Wright has already presupposed *his* knowledge of the structure of class interests, such that *he* knows what is and what is not "in the interests of the working class." And yet he has previously confessed inability to decide "true interests" from "false interests."

Wright's allegiance to an abstract theorization of the labor process grounded in the "rational actor" of bourgeois social theory grounds the way in which "class content" of consciousness has first been defined in terms of "class pertinent effects," and then these effects themselves defined in terms of an attitude scale measuring "pro" or "anti" worker attitudes. Given his general argument regarding the constitution of knowledge and consciousness, and unable to account for the most important dimensions of social practice (e.g., personality structure, hidden psychological mechanisms, cultural effects, objective interests), Wright has failed consistently to produce his dependent variable.

Amazingly, despite the unresolved problems confronting his argument, Wright not only continues his discussion but specifies in even greater detail the "elements" that compose "consciousness." "Whenever people make conscious choices," according to Wright, "three dimensions of subjectivity are implicated" (ibid., 246-247). First, the perception of alternatives. This involves "the subjective perception of what possibilities exist." "Class consciousness, in these terms involves the ways in which the perceptions of alternatives have a class content and are thus consequential for class actions" (ibid., 247).

The second dimension of subjectivity consists in "theories of consequences." "Class consciousness, in these terms, revolves around the ways in which the theories people hold shape the choices they make around class practices" (ibid.). And finally, "People have preferences." "Class consciousness, in these terms, revolves around the subjective specification of class interests" (ibid.).

What has been argued previously can be brought to bear even more heavily on Wright's bourgeois rationalist three-dimensional subjectivity. First, Wright's dissection of consciousness into perception of alternatives, theories of consequences, and preference formation identically corresponds with the standard discriminations of "rational action" in neo-Kantian academic social science, namely, factual observation, theoretical explanation, and preference-value orientation. Furthermore, Wright explicitly relies on a fact-value distinction. This distinction, as I later argue, is not consistent with a Marxist practice of subjectivity. While the separation of facts from preferences (grounded in pure logic as science of "the is" and ethics as doctrine of "the ought") is a sine qua non of mainstream social science, from the standpoint of a Marxist practice of the labor process, the production of history and knowledges of history is inescapably an indivisible and unified practice of the *practical-ethical*. Marx's argument is directed against precisely this practice of pure abstract logic and the similarly ahistorical ethical doctrines of metaphysics grounded in the alienated practice of labor as abstract mental labor.

Third, Wright's definition of "false consciousness" based in this schema has nothing at all in common with a Marxist practice of false consciousness. Wright's practice is rooted in a pre-Marxist metaphysical tradition that defined (and continues to define) knowledge in representational terms. Knowledge, according to this argument, is a *representation* of a world external to and noncontingent on human subjectivities. From this standpoint, the mind functions as a mirror[6] accurately reflecting and representing objectivities conceived as external to the subject. Given these premises of an external world to be discovered and the distorting impact that values allegedly have on efforts of accurate representation, the separation of preferences from observation and theorization is fundamental.

Wright defines "false consciousness" in terms of observation and theorization in the following way: "actors may make choices under false information, with distorted perceptions of alternative possibilities and with incorrect theories of the effects of their choices (ibid., 248). He continues: "In these ways it is fairly clear what the 'falsity' of consciousness means, although it may not be so easy to establish what 'true' consciousness actually is in these cases" (ibid.).

How can Wright establish what constitutes *false* information, *distorted* perceptions, and *incorrect* theories if, in each case, there is no standard of truth? Does not "false," "distorted," and "incorrect" already presuppose notions of truth, nondistortion, and correctness from which deviations can be judged? As in the previous argument regarding "true" interests, if Wright is unable to specify what "true" information is, he surely cannot discriminate between true and false information. Furthermore, the basis for his entire "empirical investigation" is precisely the claim that *he* supposedly knows what "true information" is — "what the data say."

Wright does not overcome this relativism. Just as he attempts to avoid the issue of "true" interests, he does the same for "the problem" of "true consciousness." He anonymously authorizes his claim to truth by silently invoking the objective standards that must be presupposed in his discussion of class consciousness. This could never logically arise from the conditions that confront Wright's "rational actor." As I later show, it is based in a *special* (i.e., scientific) theory of the labor process to be found in *Classes.*

Wright's practice of "objective interests" provides a point of departure for critiquing the implicit fact-value distinction at the core of his practice of class consciousness. I make the claim that it is Wright's separation of knowledge (i.e., "true" information, "true" observation, "true" theorization) from preference formation that produces the hypothetical situation whereby one may indeed possess a perfect knowledge of one's oppression but, simultaneously, no desire to overthrow it. I refer to this real possibility rooted in Wright's maintenance of a distinction between a science of "the is" and a doctrine of "the ought" (knowledge and preference), as "the specter of the masochistic proletariat." It is not just the logic of separating facts from values but also Wright's claim that perfect knowledge of the facts may exist without knowledge of real class interests. In other words, both the false separation of facts and values and the primacy accorded to knowledge of facticities sets up the terms of this potential masochism. As we shall see, to avert this disaster Wright develops a theory of human nature and, in so doing, creates a universalistic-essentialist nature that is both anti-Marxist and, on its own terms, unknowable. The implications of such a construction will be explored.

Wright begins by claiming the following:

> When Marxists talk about "objective interests" they are, in effect, saying that there are cases when choices can be made in which the actor has correct information and correct theories, but distorted subjective understanding of their *interests,* that is of the preferences they attach to different possible courses of action. (Ibid.)

Given Wright's fact-value distinction and his claim that interests have an "objective material basis" in the class structure itself, Wright is here claiming that there can be a situation where *I may know* that I am exploited *but not prefer* to be free. The absence of this preference for freedom is a function of what Wright terms "distorted preferences."

There "are two basic senses," according to Wright, "in which we can say that a person has a distorted understanding of their true interests. The first, and simplest, is when what a person 'really wants' is blocked psychologically through some kind of mechanism" (ibid.).

According to Wright, the

> block in question is a real mechanism, obstructing awareness of preferences/wants that actually exist in the person's subjectivity. If we understand the operation of such psychological obstructions, then we can say something about the character of the resulting distortions. (Ibid.)

The alternative to this approach, according to Wright, is one that historicalizes preference formation.

> The second way in which we can talk about distorted preferences does not imply that the undistorted preferences are actually present in the individuals subjectivity, only buried deep in the unconscious waiting to be uncovered. The second sense allows for the possibility that the distortion-mechanism operates at the level of the very formation of preferences in the first place. The obstruction, in a sense, is biographically historical. (Ibid.)

In this second sense, unlike the first, there is no potential preference for liberation merely waiting to be actualized. While it remains the case that facts are still practiced as separate from values, these values are historicalized. This historicalization of preference would be far more consistent with a Marxist materialism, since it attempts to situate the production of ethical activity firmly within the process of historical self-objectification.

Wright ahistoricizes preference determination in the first approach. Insulated from any social relations of production and labor process, this interest is supposedly "actually present . . . only buried deep in the unconscious waiting to be uncovered" (ibid.). This radically ahistorical and psychologistic practice of objective interests apparently preserves the possibility that Wright's subject *may* overcome victimization; *may* yet demand freedom; *may* attain to objective knowledge of what he/she "really wants."

Wright asserts there "are advantages and disadvantages with each of these approaches."

> The first has the advantage of being much more tractable and potentially open to empirical investigation. It is limited, however, in its ability to

contend with the deepest kinds of effects cultural
practices may have on the subjectivities of the actors. (Ibid., 249.)

"The second alternative," Wright argues, "suffers from an
almost inevitable speculative quality that may have a crucial
critical function but which renders the concept very problematic
within scientific explanations" (ibid.).

From these two evaluations of the strengths and weaknesses
of each approach, Wright concludes: "I will therefore adopt the
first sense of distortions of interests, acknowledging the way in
which it narrows the field of vision of the problems that can be
addressed" (ibid.).

There are at least two fundamental criticisms I have concerning the claims Wright is here defending. First, the advantages and disadvantages of each approach were considered in
terms of their openness to empirical investigation and scientific
explanation. Even though Wright agrees that the second approach
serves a "crucial critical function," he dismisses it on the grounds of
overspeculativeness and nonamenability for scientific explanation. Is Wright here implying that something that provides a
crucial critical function is somehow antiscientific and that
bourgeois social science is superior to critique with respect to
providing explanation? The point remains, How can something
provide a "crucial critical function" and not be worthy of any
further comment by Wright? What function? Crucial for what,
for whom?

Second, how can the first approach be tractable to empirical
investigation, if by definition, it is severely constrained from
contending "with the deepest kinds of effects cultural practices
may have on the subjectivities of actors"? These were argued to
be discursively inaccessible to consciousness, yet Wright
defends the first approach on the grounds of greater probability
of successful empirical investigation. Does Wright mean to imply

that the unconscious domain protects the possibility of empirical social science, whereas historicalized preference formation destroys that possibility?

Given this definition of distorted preferences as "subjective obstructions to understanding interests one actually holds," Wright argues, "we can begin to talk about the 'true' interests attached to a person by virtue of their incumbency in a class location, and the corresponding distortion of those interests" (ibid.). It appears, according to this claim, that externally determined interests are imputed to a *Trager*-subject irrespective of that individual's subjective state. Incumbency, not an ahistorical psyche, is the external determinant of one's interests. A psychologically unconscious distorting mechanism would then operate only to deny the rational realization of these objectively given and externally imputed interests.

Wright goes on to defend, however, what amounts to a bourgeois theory of the innate universal nature of humankind. Consider the following extraordinary claim:

> My argument will be based on an assertion about a certain kind of preference, which I believe people in general hold even if they are not consciously aware of it, namely an interest in expanding their capacity to make choices and act upon them. This preference may be blocked, but "deep down inside" people in general have a desire for freedom and autonomy. Insofar as the actual capacity that individuals have to make choices and act upon them—their real freedom—is shaped systematically by their positions in the class structure, they have objective class interests based on this real interest in freedom. (Ibid.)

This incredible position, as far away from Marxism as any pre-Marxist bourgeois humanism could be, must be considered in detail. Where does Wright obtain his "assertion about a certain kind of preference," namely, "an interest in expanding their capacity to make choices and act upon them?" On the one hand, Wright earlier claimed that objective interests reside in the location, not the incumbent, only attaching themselves by virtue of locational incumbency. But why should freedom and choice be the true interests attached to individuals locked in a class structure, rather than docility, servility, and vice? What guarantees that locational incumbency generates a desire for autonomy? On the other hand, Wright claims that "people in general" have this "certain kind of preference." What does Wright mean by "people in general"? Does this include both the capitalist class and the working class? Is not this just one of those metaphysical abstractions, like "Man" and "Nature," that Marx railed against because of their ahistorical, abstract, and idealist character?

If class location is supposed to attach an interest to persons by virtue of incumbency, how can "people in general" have identical interests in freedom and autonomy? They can express identity only if in the abstract they are identically located — in short, only if we abstract from concrete self-objectification to create these "people in general." This is a humanist-essentialist construction of freedom that views the desire for freedom as something dormant within "people in general," regardless of whether "they are . . . consciously aware of it." As Marx claimed in the *Theses on Feuerbach* (Marx and Engels 1976),

> Feuerbach resolves the essence of religion into the essence of man. But the essence of man is no abstraction inherent in each single individual. In its reality it is the ensemble of social relations. Feuerbach, who does not enter upon a criticism of this real essence, is hence obliged: 1. To abstract from the historical process and to define the religious sentiment regarded by itself, and to presuppose an abstract — *isolated* — human   individual. 2. The

essence of man, therefore, can with him be regarded only as "species," as an inner, mute, general character which unites the many individuals only *in a natural way.* (Pp. 7-8.)

What does Wright mean by the claim that "'deep down inside' people in general have a desire for freedom and autonomy"? Is he here referring to his earlier postulation of "will" as the key to discursive awareness and true knowledge? Is it "will" or some similar version of Kantian moral agency that preserves and energizes this desire for freedom and autonomy (thus declaring Enlightenment humanist war on medeival theologically based heteronomy), and all this despite concrete determination of capacities within determinate conditions of labor?

Wright refers to Andrew Levine as an influential source for this discussion of freedom, but even Levine's argument does not seem to authorize Wright's particular construction of moral agency. Though Levine seems part of the abstract analytical movement in Marxism, he does not postulate a universalist conclusion for socialist freedom.

If we count individuals equally in determinations of social well-being, as the dominant political culture would have us do, it would follow that freedom would be advanced by promoting the freedom of the many, *even if need be at the expense of the few.* Socialism, in so far as it equalizes access to the means for realizing ends, would have precisely this effect. (Levine 1984, 33; italics added.)

For Levine, freedom is gained depending on one's relation to control over the labor process and means of production. This is not Wright's argument, even though Levine dedicated his latest book to Wright, and Wright credits Levine for this part of his argument. Levine's sense of freedom would be "biographically historical" rather than "abstract-essentialist."

What does Wright mean by the expression "deep down inside"? He seems to imply the domain of the unconscious processes and mechanisms unavailable to conscious intentionality. But even though this mysterious principle may function to birth impulses toward freedom, in its own terms, it can not be proven to exist. It can only be an indemonstrable presupposition.

This presupposition, moreover, does not explain its own appearance except through Wright's invocation to "believe." Using faith to reveal the existence of freedom clearly contradicts Wright's defense of this approach on the grounds of its amenability for empirical investigation. Unfortunately for Wright, this places him back in the theological camp. Belief in something "deep down inside," also contradicts Wright's previous claim that interests are a function of locational incumbency. Like "people in general," the realm of the "deep down inside" is generic to *all* who exist as Wright's egoistic individual.

Finally, how can Wright *know* this ahistorical principle that is generic to "people in general," if he himself exists as this egoistic actor? How does Wright propose to overcome his own concrete, historical, cultural incumbency in order to posit what is, by definition and logical operation within his argument, a universal, transhistorical, transclass object? How can a contingent subject know a universal essentialist object? The failure to address these difficulties is tantamount to eliminating the argument put forth in defense of the existence of real "objective interests."

"The specter of the masochistic proletariat" is avoided by Wright through the use of such metaphysical devices. Faced with the apparent end of "freedom," given that interests may be inescapably subjective and "biographically historical" within the terms of a fact-value distinction, Wright was able to preserve liberty only by locking it "deep down inside," even if the acting subject is unaware of this.

Posited as superior to other theorizations based on alleged ease of empirical investigation, its main strength in fact comes from its capacity to sustain Kantian moral agency. Certainly Wright has admitted (and I have demonstrated) the inferiority of his approach to class consciousness vis-a-vis problems of accounting for deep cultural practices, unconscious mechanisms, and the like.

Wright defined his mission, however, as an effort to "examine the empirical relation between class structure and an attitudinal measure of class consciousness."

I have attempted to demonstrate both the necessity of Wright's construction and its impossibility for producing a knowledge of class structure in terms of such a subjectivity. Such a knowledge can never arise, since it rests on the presupposition of a radical duality between subject and object. One of the many consequences has been the fruitless effort to argue a notion of "objective interests" rooted in a theory of human nature.

Wright's efforts directed at grounding a truthful knowledge of class structure cannot yield results in these terms. In chapter 3 I argue that Wright seeks to construct a different subject and labor process that can overcome such difficulties. While it is not original to Wright's latest book, nor to his making of Marxism, it is crucial for his argument on class structure.

Notes

1. The brevity of treatment accorded this "rational choice" or "methodological individualist" standpoint must suffice for purposes of present argumentation. The emerging pervasiveness of this standpoint as strategic response to so-called crises within both bourgeois social science and variants of Marxism warrants far more discussion than that produced here. Wright's particular usage of this framework for producing his argument in *Classes* provides the focus for present efforts. For a recent, and in

my view most uncritical, review of this trend in Anglo-American Marxism see Carling (1986). Also see Burawoy (1986) for an important yet unfortunately sociologized and superficial critique of Elster (1985).

2. Adam Przeworski (1982), in the most ecstatic terms, also declares his allegiance to this practice of abstract individualism. See his "The Ethical Materialism of John Roemer" where he declares "Methodological Individualism" to be "a revolutionary breakthrough for the Marxist method" (p. 306). His final sentence sanctions this "revolutionary breakthrough" with an unequivocal clarion call: "Let me join in the pleas for a methodological individualism" (p. 313).

3. For Wright's explicit defense of functional explanation in social theory, see entire "Methodological Introduction" (1979a) but especially p.14, note 6. His position, though modified in "Giddens' Critique of Marxism" (1983a, 16-17) is based on a modified claim that "it is possible to identify some social contexts within which full-fledged functional explanations are possible in social science."

4. See Wright's "Giddens' Critique of Marxism" (1983a, 15) for an expression of this crisis of functional explanation in the works of "Althusser and other 'structuralist Marxists,'" and, most especially, the then recent criticisms of G.A. Cohen's book, *Karl Marx's Theory of History: A Defense.*

5. For example, see Elster's (1985, 18-22) discussion of "internal psychic mechanisms" and "cognitive psychology" under the heading "Subintentional Causality." For examples of moral philosophy, in the metaphysical sense of the term, see Roemer's (1982a, 288-299) advocacy of "A Sociology of Injustice." See also Andrew Levine (1984) for an example of liberalist-based idealist ethics.

6. For a non-Marxist but intriguing discussion of this assumption of classical Western metaphysics, see Rorty (1979).

Chapter 3   "Theoretical Practice" and the "Class in Itself"

Wright's failure to ground a knowledge of class structure within the terms of his construction of consciousness and class consciousness having been demonstrated, this chapter is organized as follows. I attempt to argue that Wright's particular practice of the "class in itself"/"class for itself" distinction, already implied in his previous discussion of class consciousness, prevents him from grounding a knowledge of class structure. This "class in itself," as Wright produces it, is in fact merely the abstract, externalized counterpart to his similarly abstract "rational actor." Since no concrete process of self-objectification has been argued, Wright is led to characterize this structure in terms of externalized abstract properties.

The problem that arises, one that is endemic to this kind of dualism between agent and structure, is that Wright can never build a bridge between this subject and its object. Instead of objectivity being understood as an objectification of social relations, and subjectivity being precisely this active process of self-objectification under conditions of previously objectified social relations, Wright attempts to unite an abstract "rational actor" with an equally abstract "class structure." Since Wright does not ground a knowledge of class within the active process of a class' own self-objectification, he is led to abstract from this process and hypothesize what these mysterious elements of "class in itself" must be. This leads to a situation of radical relativism that among other things, undermines Wright's efforts to authorize his concept of class structure.

The thrust of chapter 3 is to demonstrate the ways in which Wright attempts to overcome this radical relativism by postulating a special theory of the labor process grounded in a particular self-understanding and practice of "science." Wright's practice of science cannot be defended in its own terms because of the inconsistencies and contradictions plaguing Wright's grounding. Three of Wright's many insufficient suppositions are critiqued here: his particular defense of the uniqueness of scientific practice (i.e., scientific labor, scientific concepts); his practice of the boundary between the conceptual and the empirical; and his specification of the ways in which certain "conceptual constraints" operate to constrain his concept. Ultimately, Wright fails to authorize his concept of class structure because of the insurmountability of these problems plaguing his work.

Fundamental to Wright's project of class structure analysis is the distinction between a "class in itself" and a "class for itself," where the former is understood to be "objective," "really there," and "actual" because of its quality of being external to the concrete subjectivities of individuals who may occupy it. There are numerous examples of Wright's claim to maintain this distinction. For example, in chapter 7 of *Classes,* Wright (1985b) claims that the first general premise underlying his empirical investigation is this:

> The material interests rooted in exploitation relations and thus linked to class structure are real: they exist independently of the concrete subjectivities and personal characteristics of the incumbents of class location (Pp. 250-251.)

According to Wright, these are "based in the objective properties of the class structure itself." In chapter 2, Wright makes extensive reference to this distinction:

> It simply means that classes have a structural existence which is irreducible to the kinds of collective

> organizations which develop historically (class forma-
> tions), the class ideologies held by individuals and
> organizations (class consciousness) or the forms of
> conflict engaged in by individuals as class members or
> by class organizations (class struggle), and that such
> class structures impose basic constraints on these
> other elements in the concept of class. (Ibid., 28.)

Wright authorizes this claim by saying, "Most Marxists. . . implicitly or explicitly incorporate such distinctions within their
class analysis." Furthermore, when they do so

> Class structure is viewed in one way or another as
> the "basic" determinant of the other three elements,
> at least in the sense of setting the limits of possible
> variation of class formation, class consciousness
> and class struggle. (ibid.)

While Wright has authorized his class analysis in terms of a
class structure that is both fundamental to other modes of class
existence (i.e., formation, struggle, consciousness) and objectively external to individual subjectivities, his concept of class
structure remains mysteriously abstract. For example, in chapter 1
of *Classes,* Wright attempts to approach the question "What
constitutes class structure?" by offering the following vague
claims. Class structure is produced when "the social organization
of production determines a structure of 'empty places' in class
relations, places filled by people."[1] Or, class structure is "the
structure of social relations into which individuals (or, in some
cases, families) enter which determine their class interests." He
claims that class analysis is supposed to produce an "abstract
structural account of classes."

A claim made in "The American Class Structure" (1982, 711),
is unequivocal with respect to this distinction: In a discussion on
the question of constructing a typology of class, Wright offers

us the possibility of two separate projects, one in which "typology is strictly a typology of class structure ('class-in-itself')" and another in which "classes [are] organized as collective actors in class struggle ('class-for-itself')." In *Classes,* Wright similarly claims that whereas analysis of class structure deals with the "class structure as such," analysis of class formation involves "the ways in which people within class structures become organized into collectivities engaged in struggle" (Wright 1985b, 6).

Not only has Wright maintained an extremely abstract conception of what this class structure might be, he has failed to construct an understanding of the relationship between this structure—as external to subjectivities—and its occupants, who are by definition internal to the structure. Is the class structure totally independent of those who occupy it? According to Wright:

> The problem of properly describing the relationship between flesh-and-blood human individuals and social relations has been the object of protracted and often obscure debates in sociology. It is often argued that since social relations would not exist if all human individuals within those relations ceased to exist, it therefore makes no sense to distinguish the structure from the individuals within the structure. (Ibid., 17.)

What Wright has raised here as "protracted and often obscure debates" is the possibility that his entire project is groundless. This would certainly be the case, given the possible absence of an independent structure warranting a class analysis. This admission problematizes the alleged project at the heart of *Classes,* namely, Wright's attempt at "elaborating a rigourous map of the concrete social structure" (ibid., 7). Or, again to "provide a set of precise concepts for decoding rigourously the structural basis of most of those categories" (ibid.).

Let us consider Wright's attempted solution in more detail. Wright tries to develop his own understanding of the relationship between structure and the individuals occupying it, and in so doing he claims:

> The formulation I have adopted does not give social relations an existence independent of people as such, but does give them an existence independent of particular persons. Stated differently: you can change all of the actual individuals in a factory in the course of a generation and yet the class structure of the factory could remain the same. (Ibid., 17.)

I first critique the problems inherent in this "solution" and then go on to a more general critique of the possibility that Wright can even develop a knowledge of "class structure" in the terms he has set. What must be possible in order for one to be able to "change all of the actual individuals in a factory in the course of a generation and yet the class structure of the factory could be the same"? How can we conceive of different *individuals over time* (and presumably, space) reproducing identical structures — structures without difference? Do not we have to presuppose no dependence of individuals on class structure? In fact, what must be presupposed is what Wright himself said, an *in*dependence, that is, an absence of relation that is a relation of absence, and vice versa. The "class structure" is in no way affected by what any particular person does or does not do, which means that particular persons, despite Wright's current allegiance to a "rational actor" subject, do not even reproduce class structure! That very peculiar relation of absence is an absence of relation that yields the appearance of a class structure that exists *externally* to each and every individual who *occupies* a *position within it*. In this respect, structure is reproducible as identical structure irrespective of individual class practices.

Furthermore, Wright cannot account for social change. If class structure is identically reproducible, then what we are really referring to is a static abstraction unaffected by "the course of a generation." For a generation to practice under atemporal-aspatial circumstances would be to contradict the meaning of "generation." Yet for a generation of people to fail to generate a new class structure is to do precisely that. Wright's practice of "class structure" as an abstract structural constraint on an already constituted "rational actor" rather than as an objec-tification of a capitalist labor process is precisely what is at issue here.

Perhaps Wright is referring to the notion that irrespective of the *individuals* who occupy a class structure, it still remains a *class* structure. Whether Ms. X or Mr. Y are incumbents of class structure Z, they must both operate according to this common term. This common term would serve effectively to dissolve the particular subjective into the real objective structure. It also seems to follow, however, that if you take away X or Y, Wright still has Z.

But what does the class structure look like when X and Y are absent from the scene? When Wright defines the class structure with the locational metaphor "empty places," this is a postulation of pure form without content, pure empty spatiality. Certainly to arrive at a notion of "places without people" is to practice an alienated self-consciousness that conceives of everyone else to be gone, yet the thinker still able to posit this state of absentia. Marx alludes to this abstractionist's predicament when he claims:

> Or if you want to hold onto your abstraction, then
> be consistent, and if you think of man and nature as
> non-existent, then think of yourself as non-existent,
> for you too are surely nature and man. Don't think,
> don't ask me, for as soon as you think and ask, your
> abstraction from the existence of nature and man
> has no meaning. Or are you such an egotist that you

conceive everything as nothing, and yet want your-
self to exist? (Marx and Engels 1975, 305.)

Athough Marx's charge is leveled at those who attempt to debate
the "origins" of "Man" and "Nature," the critique can be
directed at Wright's practice of abstracting social practice to arrive at asocial, ahistorical "structures."

Wright tries to avoid positing this specter of abstract thought,
by claiming that "The formulation . . . adopted does not give
social relations an existence independent of people as such."
The reference to "people as such," however, does not fare much
better than reference to "particular persons." To refer to "people as
such" is to presuppose a notion of "class structure as such." Far
from being dependent on "people as such" for its definition, this
"class structure as such" would be defined through a relation of
absence from such people. The "as such" here indicates the abstract
general properties of a "class in itself" devoid of any concrete
particularities or specific class practices. This not only refutes
Wright's claim that class structure is dependent on people for its
existence, it reproduces its externality from such people. Furthermore, Wright's use of "people as such" replaces concrete
class practices with that *abstract* generality of "man" or
"humanity," etc. Otherwise, the "as such" merely idles (i.e.,
"people as people").

Finally, and most crucial, Wright's central premise of class
analysis seems to dissipate by the suggestion that "people as
such" are not independent of the class structure. Wright has
maintained throughout his project of class structure analysis the
possibility and necessity of creating distinctions between "class
structure" (i.e., an abstract relation consisting of "empty
places") and the historical objectifications of class (i.e., classes
engaged in their formation, struggles, and creation of consciousness). Implied by this latest part of Wright's argument,
however, is the notion that class structure cannot be understood

"independent of people as such" and that a class analysis cannot be grounded on such a distinction.

Wright has produced an inconsistency at the very heart of his understanding of class analysis. If Wright tries to maintain a relation of externality between "class structure" and "people as such," which seemed to be the central thrust of his postulation of class structure as a set of "empty places," he must contradict this latest claim to deny such a distinction. On the other hand, if we accept Wright's later claim that class structure cannot really be theorized independently of "people as such" within social relations, the necessary grounding for class analysis (e.g., an independent structure of "empty places") seems to have been destabilized. The resolution of this inconsistency is no mere aside to Wright's argument. If the very foundation of Wright's class analysis of capitalist society is the maintenance of a distinction between its structure and its historical variations, and if this distinction collapses under close inspection, Wright's project itself seems to have no grounding. The impossibility of disclosing the boundaries of a class structure devoid of either "particular persons" or "people as such" eliminates any justification Wright may have for avoiding the self-objectification of historical class *practices* as the central basis for class analysis.

Wright's inability to specify the relation existing between the "class structure as such" and persons occupying this structure stems from an even greater weakness, namely, Wright's failure to provide a consistent grounding for his own knowledge of such a "class in itself." If, by his definition, this structure possesses objectivity by virtue of its noncontingence on and externality from the subjectivities of particular persons, how is Wright going to bridge the gap between his merely subjective knowledge and the objectivity of this "class in itself"? Let us further assume (in order to remain consistent with Wright's previous chapter 7 argument on class consciousness) that consciousness is merely an aspect of the concrete subjectivities of individual persons. Given these two assumptions—that a "class in itself" is an objectivity existing external to my subjectivity and that consciousness is an aspect of the concrete subjectivities of individuals—how does Wright (as this subjective, contingent, historical, class-formed, individual consciousness) gain a true and objective knowledge of this noncontingent, nonformed class structure? In other words, how can Wright's radically individualist and contingent consciousness attain a knowledge of "class structure" which is, by definition, external to and not dependent on his subjectivities? How can a conditioned consciousness attain knowlege of an unconditioned objectivity that resides logically external to this conditioned consciousness?

There are several grounds for denying Wright the possibility of overcoming this seemingly insuperable crisis of authority. Most important, Wright's very argument (or in this case, lack of a consistent argument) on class consciousness fails to provide the grounds enabling such a knowledge (Wright 1985, 241-251). This is a direct consequence of Wright's lack of success in formulating the necessary conditions that constitute rationality. By implication, this alone undermines the need for truth-discriminating criteria. This indeterminacy over a basis for rationality in turn leads to Wright's hopeless subjection to processes and class structures that must defy, by definition, attempts at rational comprehension.

Even if we leave aside that major problem implicating Wright's formulation of class consciousness, there still remain other central obstacles barring Wright's production of a knowledge of class structure. Aside from his initial abstract discussion of "empty places," Wright never really discusses how it is that he arrives at this notion of "class structure." While he may argue that "class structure" must simply be thought of as a central premise of Marxism, in the terms of his argument, he can only posit a particular perspective or interpretation of what that structure might be. Wright cannot posit class structure as anything other than his *interpretation* of that structure unless he claims to be immune from the conditions of consciousness he himself has constructed. The fact is, Wright cannot discover the class structure; therefore, he presupposes it in vague allusions that refer only to general features. Abstract presuppositions, even Wright should agree, are a far cry from objective knowledge.

Furthermore, how would Wright even begin to discriminate among rival claims vis-á-vis its real objective properties? What criteria will be used to adjudicate between Ms. X's and Mr. Y's definitions of class structure? As in the case of his argument concerning class consciousness, there are two possibilities, and *both* fall short of Wright's claim to know the objective class structure. On the one hand, he can rely on external criteria based in the class structure itself. But that is impermissible unless Wright engages in presupposing what must be proven, namely, that those external criteria really are constitutive of the class structure. On the other hand, we can use individual criteria to judge rival claims about the real class structure. But what provides his basis for discriminating among competing claims? How does he go about claiming that definition X is superior to definition Y? And will not his capacity to discriminate between X and Y presuppose a "real object," external to all particular interpretations, from which these can be judged as mere interpretations? In other words, Wright's interpretationism necessarily presupposes a unified object by which interpretations can be just that, partial perceptions of the real object. By definition, however, an interpretivist framework cannot posit the real object (class structure), since it can be accessed only as a partial, necessarily conditioned perspective.

The distinction between the "in itself" and the "for itself," and the controversy whether and how Marxists accept it, reject it, or deny that Marx ever made it,[2] has a decided impact on how one practices a class analysis. The stabilization provided by Wright's particular rendering of the category "class in itself" (or "class as such") allows, for example, for the creation of a typological map that claims to represent, however abstractly, the "in itself." In fact, this particular practice of "class in itself" has allowed Wright the liberty of completely abstracting from a class' conscious being and actually postulating this process of abstraction as a condition for class analysis itself! The very possibility of abstracting class from its process of self-objectification and neatly pigeonholing it into a Weberian-like typological schema rests on the maintenance of this distinction.

Wright's failure to produce a true and necessary knowledge of class structure within the terms of his construction of class consciousness has not led him to abandonment of the project. Instead, Wright has relied on what amounts to a *special* consciousness—one that is alleged to overcome the inevitable relativism that heretofore plagues his grounding. It is to the special theory of the labor process and its unique grounding in a special consciousness that I now turn.

The principal claim I argue is that Wright attempts to overcome the epistemological relativism of his position through grounding in a particular practice of "scientia"—one very much bound up with Wright's Althusserian and post-Althusserian "realist" views on what constitutes proper method within Marxism. Wright in effect argues that this scientific labor process (most especially, its unique conceptual products) is alone capable of producing an accurate knowledge of the real class structure. I attempt to argue that while Marx certainly considered his work scientific in the sense that it led to a truer practice of the labor process, Wright's practice of science is based in an alienated non-Marxist practice of the labor process.

While an almost fetishistic attachment to a particular rendering and practice of scientific authority runs through all of Wright's work,[3] I concentrate specifically on the argument made in *Classes*. References to Wright's practice of science in other works are used only as they relate to this argument.

It is crucial to keep in mind Wright's basic premise—that a real class structure exists independent of the subjectivities of persons (most especially, the subjectivity of the "theorist" or "class analyst"). Because of this, the "real," "actual," "objective" structure, according to Wright, can be known only as a concept. For example, in the statement, "Class is X," the "is X" is merely a definition, while "class" is the actual, independent, real object behind our definition of it. In fact, "class" here is the *idea* of class, an ideal existence that exists independent of any particular predication of what this class might be (its real boundary, structure, etc.). The significance of Wright's practice of "the concept" comes then from the fact that "concepts are peculiar kinds of hypotheses: hypotheses about the boundary criteria of real mechanisms" (Wright 1985b, 131-132).

Wright's class structure analysis consists in giving this real class structure "its concept," or "its definition," and proving that his concept (presented in chapters 3 and 4 of *Classes)* is an accurate *re*presentation of this objective reality.

Grounding Wright's use of the concept in this manner is a practice of "science" that sees the road to truth conditional on the production of more superior concepts. This is Kant or even Hegel speaking, but certainly not Marx. Wright claims that "if Marxist theory is at all scientific one would expect conceptual advances to have occurred in such a period" (ibid., 16). Wright is here referring to the changing scientific status of class analysis over the last hundred years of Marxist theorizing. Note Wright's reduction of the labor process (the activity of historical self-objectification through previously objectified conditions of labor) to that of merely mentalistically conceived conceptual activity and a definition of scientific progress as conceptual advance.

Because of this practice of science, these truth-bearing concepts are singled out as vessels to be purged of any researcher-theorist "imputed" subjectivities. Wright's unique practitioners (i.e., theorists) of legitimate science must be capable of conceptually penetrating[4] the essential nature of the real class structure, and to that end, he must ensure the elimination of all human bias. Characteristic of this project of purification is an understanding of human practice itself as truth distorting,[5] and along with this, extended considerations of the necessary methodology for achieving such objective scientific knowledge.[6] This debate on method is characteristic of neo-Kantian-based academic social science inasmuch as the so-called problem is one of historicity and subjectivity, or more commonly, the "problem of bias." The path to truth (given that truth is defined in the terms of a non-Marxist epistemology as agreement of knowledge with the object), then, requires eliminating contingent, value-laden historicity from "biasing" this purely *re*presentational function of scientific knowledge. Of course, in keeping with Wright's non-Marxist practice of the knowledge-production process, the real ground and tribunal for all this is that noble domain of "pure reason." But more on this later.

Authorizing this search for that unconditioned reality of pure class structure, Wright offers a definition of the "new" Marxist class analysis. Wright claims that

> while the themes in this recent work are rooted in classical Marxism, the new Marxist class analysis is distinctive in two respects: first, much of this work has attempted a level of self-conscious conceptual precision that was only rarely encountered in earlier Marxist discussions of these problems. Secondly, it has systematically tried to develop concepts and theories at the "middle level" of abstraction, less abstract than the exploration of modes of production but more abstract than the concrete investigation of the concrete situation. (Ibid., 15.)

Singling out "abstraction" and "conceptual sophistication" as definitive of the "new Marxist class analysis," Wright admits that this new analysis seeks to construct an abstract conceptual-theoretical *object for knowledge,* not a practical one. In other words, abstract conceptual mapping and not real class struggle is definitive of the "new Marxist class analysis." Not surprisingly, such a practice of the "new" is quite compatible with the neo-

Kantian Weberian-based fixations with abstract mappings and typological schemas that have and continue to occupy sociologists working squarely within the mainstream of "stratification" theory.

Three principal claims are defended throughout this section as I consider Wright's specific argument in *Classes* regarding this labor process alleged to be unique to scientific investigation and production. First, Wright cannot authorize the uniqueness of scientific products vis-á-vis other social products. Second, Wright fails to define the boundaries between the conceptual and empirical domains, and therefore fails to define "the boundary criteria of real mechanisms" (e.g., class structure). And finally, because of Wright's inability to discriminate between concepts — given his failure to establish boundaries between the empirical and conceptual realms — he is left without any possible grounding by which even to engage in his project of class structure analysis. Wright's very concept of class (chapter 3) and his discussion of its significant implications (chapter 4) cannot be arrived at, since Wright is incapable even of formulating the necessary grounding by which to arrive at this concept and its implications. In a portent of things to come, Wright immediately indicates, in the form of a disclaimer, the self-imposed superficiality regarding his discussion of scientific-conceptual matters.

> The purpose of this discussion will not be to explore in any depth the epistemological problem of the status of concepts or the alternative approaches to the problem of concept formation that various theorists have advocated, but rather, simply to make accessible the rationale for the approach that will be followed in the rest of this book. (Ibid., 19.)

Wright authorizes this conservative and uncritical approach by claiming that "a great deal of substantive debate in the Marxist tradition is couched in an idiom of debates over the methodological and philosophical principles which underlie social analysis" (ibid.). Moreover, "This has the effect of altogether displacing concern with substantive theoretical issues by a preoccupation with epistemological problems. I wish to avoid such a displacement in this book" (ibid.).

To ignore minor tributaries is one thing, but what Wright here self-consciously imposes as limitation is central to his argument. He is attempting to bracket from his class structure analysis the vital issue of grounding, just as he did in his previous arguments regarding class consciousness. Wright opens himself up to fundamental criticisms by not seriously exploring the grounds for his larger argument on class structure. Given this, Wright necessarily presupposes, in an uncritical way, certain methodological and epistemological assumptions grounding his "substantive theoretical" claims. While I reject Wright's distinction between the "theoretical-substantive" and "methodological-philosophical"—this smacks of mainstream social science and *not* Marxism—the failure of Wright's argument can be demonstrated even within these terms.

Wright begins his discussion of science in *Classes* with a section entitled "The Logic of Concept Formation." Starting the first sentence on a fruitful note by making a general claim about concepts—"Concepts are produced"—he then identifies the agents of these productions: Concepts are "produced by human beings." So far, so good. "Concepts are produced by human beings." To this point he has established that concepts—like *all* social productions—are objectifications of human labor.

Ever so subtly, however, the ground shifts and the labor process of concept formation becomes restricted at the same time that the available pool of conceptualizers begins to shrink. Wright qualifies his general claim by asserting that "this [the claim that human beings produce concepts] is true regardless of one's epistemological prejudices and methodological predilections, whether one regards concepts as cognitive mappings of real mechanisms in the world or as strictly arbitrary conventions in the imagination of the theorist" (ibid.).

The claim that the domain of concept formation should be practiced as "cognitive" or as "in the imagination of the theorist" has quickly replaced Wright's first claim, namely, that "human beings produce concepts." This remains an unexplained deduction from his first general claim. Why, then, must it be posited? Cannot concepts be practiced as objectifications of broader social relations than those implied in the relations of "theorist" to "nontheorist"? Is Wright readily willing to import the entire history of non-Marxist Western metaphysics and its presupposed grounding in "cognitive" and merely intelligible labor? In chapter 7 Wright admits that there is a legitimate alternative to practicing consciousness as the concrete subjectivities of an individual (ibid., 280 note 4), one that locates consciousness in practices implicated in all social relations. This practice of the subject would surely challenge the association of conceptual activity with the individual psyches of particular theorists.

Wright makes no mention of these difficulties and, continuing his argument, claims that concepts "are never simply given by the real world as such but are always produced through some sort of intellectual process of concept formation" (ibid.). What are the implications of this unexplained presupposition governing Wright's discussion, namely, that concept formation is an intellectual process pursued by an agent called a theorist that is constituted by cognition and/or imagination? "Theorist" is not a harmless word, given that he has narrowed the field of conceptualizers to theorizers (understood more narrowly as a specific credentialled actor within some structure of legitimacy— i.e., the theorizer as a special actor, possessing "mental" rather than "manual" dexterity), and, as we shall see, Wright engages in the reduction of conceptual labor to a particular notion of "theoretical practice."[7]

Wright unequivocally makes this reduction at the beginning of the next paragraph by claiming, "The production of concepts that figure in scientific theories takes place under a variety of constraints" (ibid.). Wright's class analysis is now defined as an intellectual-conceptual activity whose special product will be "the production of concepts that figure in scientific theories." This elitist and privileging exercise is unwarranted, unexplained, and proceeds as if requiring no justification. There is simply no discussion of what discriminates the "scientific" from the "non-scientific," or where the criteria would come from to make these discriminations.

Further augmenting Wright's privileging of scientific labor is his effort to distinguish "scientific concepts" from mere "nonscientific concepts." Wright makes a startling claim about what he considers the role and characteristics of scientific concepts. While referring to the twin risks of "theoreticism" and "empiricism," he claims:

> It should be noted that there is no absolute virtue in scientific concepts over other sorts of concepts — aesthetic concepts, moral concepts, theological concepts, etc.. Theoreticism and empiricism, defined in the above manner, are sins only with respect to the objective of producing concepts for scientific purposes i.e. concepts which can figure in explanations of the real world. (Ibid., 58.)

Encapsulated in this passage are a number of specifically non-Marxist practices. On the one hand, the distinctions between the aesthetic, moral, and scientific are not based in a Marxist practice of the labor process. In fact, these so-called conceptual distinctions correspond with the classical pre-Marxist philosophical division of reality and knowledges of reality into a science of "the is" (logic), a doctrine of "the ought" (ethics), and a doctrine of "the beautiful" (aesthetics). There is no basis in Marx's argument for making such discriminations; furthermore, Marx's argument is directed against precisely the abstract "conceptual" labor that abstracts from unified historical production to arrive at this kind of false analytical division.

On the other hand, while Wright denies "absolute virtue," he must imply "relative virtue" for scientific concepts. This is based on the allegation that they (unlike mere moral and aesthetic concepts) "can figure in explanations of the real world," but nowhere does he indicate how and why this is so. Perhaps we are to assume that Wright's particular science of "the is," being totally abstracted from questions of ethical activity and aesthetic judgement, and precisely for that reason, has provided him a vehicle for knowing the "real world." But why must this be so?

Once we destabilize the metaphysically grounded logic-ethic (fact-value) distinction, how are we to arrive at this notion of "relative superiority"? Within the terms of this distinction, it seems to make sense that science, unlike theological and other practices and productions, is concerned with explanations of this world. But is Wright really willing to accept the divides established by seventeenth-century scientific challengers of theological authority and import the terms of that challenge, willy-nilly, *as a Marxism?*

In all fairness, it is important again to note that Wright's fascination with "concepts" is not really grounded in Marxism but in a variant of scientific or philosophic "realism." This separation of ethical activity from questions of scientific explanation is in fact a necessity given that Wright is relying on a classical representational epistemology. But Marx's critique of the profoundly alienated practice of the labor process sustaining all liberalist-based views of science, morality, knowledge production, etc., is based squarely in the uprooting of these false divides of the social. His attack on the abstract mentalist labor premise that sustains these divisions simply will not uphold

Wright's antiquarian views regarding the meaning of "relative" and "absolute" virtue of scientific explanation.

Despite Wright's failure to argue the uniqueness of scientific concepts he insists on laying out in more detail the uniqueness of these productions. The next set of arguments deals with Wright's attempt to establish an absolute boundary between the realms of the conceptual and the empirical. Given the representational role that Wright's "concept" is supposed to fulfill, not only must he be able to discriminate his class concept from mere false representations, dreamworlds, and imagination, the data must in some real sense "adjudicate" the validity of his conceptual labor. This discussion involves two levels of argumentation, one establishing general boundaries separating the conceptual from the empirical, and a second regarding the operation of "specific constraints" on his particular concept of class.

Central to Wright's argument is the notion of "constraints." Since concept production has been defined in terms of the cognition, imagination, and intellection of theorists, Wright discusses the mechanisms that "constrain" and thus set boundaries on the theoretical imagination. These do the same work for Wright as they once did for Descartes when confronting the question "How do I know that I'm not merely dreaming all of this class structure stuff"? These constraints allegedly prevent Wright's imagination from running wild and producing any kind of concept it "wills." In short, they allow Wright to discriminate between fantasia and the "real mechanisms of the world."

Wright defines "constraints" in the following way.

> By "constraints" I mean that in any given situation there is only a limited range of possible concepts that can be produced; while concepts are produced by the human imagination they are not produced in a completely free and unstructured manner which makes anything possible. (ibid., 20.)

According to Wright there are two kinds of constraints — "theoretical and empirical constraints." Once again, as with Wright's previous separation of theory from philosophy and methodology, a model of mainstream academic social science (premised in a radical separation between subject (theoretical) and object (empirical), grounds the specification of "constraints."

This separation is further grounded in a classical practice of the "theorics" and "empirics." The "theoric" — a classical term designating the rational, mindful activity of looking out upon and contemplating the essence of an external, already constituted being, meaning, and cause — by definition implies contemplative practice as its mode of existence and abstract thinking as solely constitutive of the historical labor process. It was precisely this abstract, contemplative practice that Marx excoriated as the practice of abstract materialism, which is in fact a form of idealism.

As for the classical "empiric," this referred to those charlatans and quacks who followed the empirical method — conceived as an atheoretical, experiential-observational-based method concerned to ameliorate rather than explain the painful symptoms of disease or illness. In its medically based classical usage it can be a pejorative reference to persons unconcerned with causality and rational comprehension of worldly data.

Finally, to specify constraint in terms of the "theoric" versus "empiric" separation presupposes both a mind-body dualism — premised in a *homo duplex* sanctioning the division of the mind into two separate faculties, a faculty of intelligibility (conceptual) and a faculty of sensibility (empirical) — and subject-object dualism, where the object's "real" content has an actuality independent of any particular formation (through consciousness) of that content.

Wright does not engage (let alone indicate any knowledge of) Marx's critique of classical contemplative materialism, and instead authorizes these so-called conceptual and theoretical constraints on the human imagination. Reflecting this uncritical posture, *Classes* itself is organized by these classical boundaries; Part I deals with "Conceptual Issues" and Part II is entitled "Empirical Investigations." Wright's *Class Structure and Income Determination* (1979b) practices the same categorization; Part I is entitled "Theoretical Perspective" and Part II, "The Empirical Investigation of Class Mediations of the Income Determination Process." While this may strike readers of my argument against Wright as a petty concern, to me it is just another example of how sociologism has replaced Marxism as a mode even of textual production.

Wright seems totally unaware that "concepts" — practiced as those unique objectifications of "intelligible" labor — are the linchpin of idealist Western metaphysics. Within this traditional practice, "intellection," as a faculty of the "mind," produces "concepts" considered *superior to* other human productions. Concepts in metaphysics function to encapsulate the "ideas" produced by the "mind."[8] This celebration of the powers of pure unfettered reason in terms of (1) what distinguishes us from nonhuman nature; and (2) within human history, from those humans who do not engage in scientific-theoretical intellection is standard fare in Wright's work. Consider Wright's argument on class consciousness. Why did he assert that "classes as such" are not legitimate entities worthy of measurement? First, as I argued, Wright made his construction of consciousness conditional on its future role as a dependent variable in a regression equation; hence, "class attitude" quickly replaced class practice as criterion for class consciousness. But, second, Wright also alludes to this special category called the "mind."

> But such supra-individual entities, and in particular "classes," do not have consciousness in the literal sense, since they are not the kinds of entities which have minds, which think, weigh alternatives, have preferences, etc. (Wright 1985b, 243.)

Despite these metaphysical premises, Wright engages in an elaborate discussion of theoretical and empirical constraints. There are two types of constraints.

> First, concepts have theoretical presuppositions. In some cases these presuppositions function as explicit, systematic theoretical requirements imposed on the production of a new concept; in other instances, the theoretical presuppositions act more as unconscious cognitive filters shaping what is thinkable by the theorist. In either case, such theoretical presuppositions determine, if only vaguely and implicitly, the range of possible concepts that can be produced. (Ibid., 20.)

"Scientific concepts," he continues,

> no matter how embedded in an elaborated theoretical framework are never constrained exclusively by theoretical presuppositions. They also face what can be called "empirically mediated real-world constraints," or simply "empirical constraints" for short. (Ibid.)

Wright then defines precisely what this expression means.

> This cumbersome expression—"empirically mediated real world constraint" is meant to convey two things: first, that the constraint in question comes from real mechanisms in the world, not simply from the conceptual framework of the theory; and second, that this real-world constraint operates through data gathered using the concepts of the theory. The constraint is thus empirically mediated, rather than directly imposed by "the world as it really is." (Ibid.)

In making these two assertions about "constraints," Wright creates a dualism between "the world as it really is" (the *real world* behind the mediated empirical) and "theoretical presuppositions," (concepts mediating this *real world*), which "determine, if only vaguely and implicitly, the range of possible concepts that can be produced." This creates a serious problem for his argument. If "theoretical presuppositions" are his only relationship to the "world as it really is," how can he ever posit that world, except (as Wright has) in quotations? Quotation marks are used to designate either an apparent reality which is false, the contingent nature of an undefined yet current expression, or direct quotation. Since Wright is authorizing his claim and is referring to a real, not apparent, world, quotations function in the second sense specified above. What guarantees that this empirical constraint in question "comes from real mechanism in the world, not simply from the conceptual framework itself"?

Wright's failure to guarantee this relation of "concepts" to "world" was to some extent anticipated by his discussion of the dangers involved. Wright refers to two possible pitfalls, "theoreticism" or "empiricism." "Theoreticism" is the risk of "effectively immunizing the theory from the operation of empirical constraints required by the explanatory tasks of the theory" (ibid., 21-22). On the other hand, "empiricism" is when "theory is organized in such a way that it blocks the development of such self-conscious theoretical constraints" (ibid., 22).

For the moment, let us suppose that Wright's metaphysical vocabulary is acceptable—that "theorics" and "empirics" are separate practices such that, for example, a "raw empiricism" can be actual. Furthermore, let us suppose that Wright's argument concerning the real risks of "empiricism" and "theoreticism" is warranted. How does Wright propose avoiding these risks? The costs are high, since, according to Wright, "If the methodological sins of theoreticism or empiricism are carried to extremes, then the very status of the resulting concepts as 'scientific' may be jeapordized" (ibid.).

Wright begins to indicate his "solution" to the correlated dangers of "theoreticism" and "empiricism" in a crucial note.

> The fact that real world constraints operate through concepts has sometimes led people to treat the constraint imposed by empirical investigation as identical to the general theoretical framework, since both operate, in a sense, "in thought." (Ibid., 58.)

Wright here recognizes, as did the rest of pre-Marxist dualist philosophy wrestling with the terms of this "rationalist" versus "empiricist" schema, the possible idealism of his constraints. Since concepts, for Wright, are *rational* constraints, he must be sure that his mind actually mirrors the real world. Yet can he be sure that his conclusions are not merely imaginative *false* representations of "the world as it really is"? Continuing his response to this dilemma, Wright offers a totally unsatisfactory response. Claiming that "this [referring to the possibility that the empirical is merely "in thought"] I think, is a mistake," Wright continues:

> Even though there is not a one to one relationship between the way the world "really is" and the data of an empirical investigation (since that data is gathered through pre-given concepts), the data is constrained by real mechanisms in the world. (Ibid.)

The assertion that "the data is constrained by real mechanisms in the world" does not follow (except as a possible article of faith), given Wright's previous admission that conceptual mediation is necessary and inescapable for knowing the "world as it really is." If the world can only be given through "pre-given concepts," and if these are by definition inescapable for scientific investigation, then how can Wright discriminate between rival concepts based on the "really there" criteria of this world?

Since within the terms of Wright's practice of knowledge production there is no "is" that is not already "is conceptual,"
Wright cannot establish any correspondence between the "world"
and its "concept." The world cannot adjudicate these *for us,*
since it is a level of reality that we can only know conceptually.
The only correspondence we have is the one Wright fallaciously
posits between this assumed reality, which he is not privileged to
know, and his concept, which he has not yet established a
grounding for. How does he know that "real mechanisms in the
world" really cause our true knowledge of this world and not
simply our false imagination? Concluding this note, Wright
claims in defense:

> If the world were different, the data would be dif-
> ferent, just as the data would be different if the con-
> cepts were different. This implies that the empirical
> constraint on concept formation—the constraint
> imposed by the fact that concepts must directly or
> indirectly figure in explanations of empirical
> phenomena—can be viewed as a mediated constraint
> of the real world itself. (Ibid.)

This is a totally unwarranted conclusion. Wright claims,
"If the world were different, the data would be different." In
itself, that is to say nothing more than that difference is all em-
bracing. Or at its worst, it is an utter tautology. Since "data" are
worldly, Wright is really claiming that "if the data were different the data would be different" or similarly, "if the world
were different the world would be different." If we are Martians
who live on Mars instead of earthlings who live on earth, then
we can expect Martian data instead of earthly data.

Beyond being a simple claim to a relation of different data
to different worlds, and given Wright's role as bearer of the
"concept," Wright cannot posit how or when this difference oc-
curs. Since, by definition, "the world" exists only through his

concepts, he can never establish that different concepts are a function of different worlds. He can only posit that concepts exist. They may be of the same world, they may be totally imaginary, they may be of different worlds. But how can Wright discriminate between different worlds? He cannot. So while Wright insists there exists some correspondence between "data" and "world," he cannot logically argue that it is a function of a different world — only that it is a function of "pre-given concepts." But Wright claims far more than this. He concludes that this "implies that the empirical constraint on concept formation . . . can be viewed as a mediated constraint of the real world itself."

There is no basis whatsoever, beyond mere speculation, that Wright's concept is being constrained by "the real world itself." Or, even if there were such "constraints," in what way they might operate; yet he presumes a very specific meaning to the operation of "constraints." There are simply no guarantees for constraint. Unable to demonstrate the boundary between the "conceptual" and the "empirical," Wright is left with what he warned against — the reality of both "theoreticism" and "empiricism." In short, Wright has simply reproduced the problem of subject-object dualism inherent in pre-Marxist philosophy and its attendant conclusion in epistemological relativism.

Wright proceeds to develop specific "conceptual constraints" operative in the production of his class concept despite his failure to establish the uniqueness of scientific concepts and the necessary boundaries distinguishing "conceptual" and "empirical" worlds. As Wright here practices the meaning and necessity of "concepts," these more specific constraints function in the same manner as "conceptual constraints" more generally. Their elaboration is considered fundamental to arriving at a "concept" of class that will accurately represent, however tenuously, the "real" properties of the "real class structure." Wright begins:

> One of the pivotal problems in any process of
> systematic concept formation is knowing what the
> theoretical constraints on the process are. In the case
> of the concept of class, there is hardly a consensus
> among Marxists as to what constitutes the general
> Marxist theory of class relations, and depending
> upon how the constraints within that general theory
> are characterized, the range of possible solutions to
> the transformation of a specific concept will be dif-
> ferent. A great deal potentially hinges, therefore, on
> precisely how those constraints are specified. (Ibid.,
> 27.)

Wright is indicating here, as in his earlier discussion of concepts, the necessity with which his knowledge of class structure
depends on a precise specification of the "constraints" on that
knowledge. Furthermore, Wright alludes to the heterogeneity
to be found among Marxists over the rules for specifying such
constraining criteria. The "great deal" Wright refers to is the
very possibility of class structure analysis. Wright sees class
structure analysis itself tied to the prospects for successful "constraint" formation. Continuing, he claims:

> The specification of the characteristics of the
> general concept of class which I will propose cannot
> be taken either as an authoritative reading of the
> classical texts of Marxism or as an account of some
> implicit majority opinion among Marxists. While I
> do feel that the theoretical conditions elaborated
> below are consistent with Marx's general usage and
> the underlying logic of many contemporary Marxist
> discussions, I will make no attempt to validate this
> claim. At a minimum, these characteristics are cen-
> tral elements within Marxist debates on the concept
> of class, even if they are not exhaustive or unconten-
> tious. (Ibid.)

According to Wright, "The task at hand, then, is to specify the constraints imposed by the *abstract* theory of classes in Marxism on the process of producing more *concrete* concepts, in this case a concrete concept capable of dealing with 'middle classes' in capitalism" (ibid). I will not here deal with Wright's claim to study the "middle classes," since a general critique of Wright's practice of "specific constraints" will be, by implication, sufficient grounds for dismissing Wright's argument about the "middle classes."

According to Wright, "Two general types of constraints are especially important: (1)constraints imposed by the explanatory role of the concept of class within the Marxist theory of society and history; and (2)constraints imposed by the structural properties of the abstract concept of class which enable it to fulfill this explanatory role in the general theory" (ibid.).

Let us first consider Wright's discussion of the "explanatory role of the concept of class within a Marxist theory of society and history." Wright asserts that "two clusters of explanatory claims for the concept of class . . . are the most important," designated by Wright as "Conceptual Constraint 1" and "Conceptual Constraint 2." The first specific conceptual constraint is the fact that "class structure imposes limits on class formation, class consciousness and class struggle" (ibid.).

He claims that "this statement implies neither that these four subconcepts of the general concept of class are definable independently of each other nor that they only have 'external' or 'contingent' interrelationships" (ibid.:27).

Wright continues:

> It simply means that classes have a structural existence which is irreducible to the kinds of collective organizations which develop historically (class formations), the class ideologies held by individuals and organizations(class consciousness) or the forms of conflict engaged in by individuals as class

members or by class organizations(class struggle),
and that such class structures impose basic constraints on these other elements in the concept of
class. (Ibid., 28.)

But there are several problems with this approach to practicing this first "conceptual constraint." It is not the fact that class
is inessential to an understanding of society and history that I
am arguing here. My argument against Wright stems from what
I consider to be his alienated practice of a class' conscious being
within this society and history. First, as demonstrated earlier in
this chapter, Wright has failed to account for how he can overcome his own "formation," "consciousness," and "struggle" in
order to posit this "class structure," which is by his account both
primary and external to Wright's own consciousness. In order
to arrive at a "class structure" — nonreducible to its historical
particularization — Wright must abstract from social practice,
his own, and attempt to gain a true knowledge of this ahistorical
structural entity. Wright himself claims that this postulation of
a structural existence for class is "not an uncontentious issue.
E.P. Thompson, for example, has argued that the structural existence of classes is largely irrelevant outside the lived experience
of actors" (ibid.). The "lived experience of actors" in this sense
can never arrive at knowledge about an external entity that is
outside these experiences. One can only arrive at this object as
an abstraction from both Wright's objectification as "theorist"
of this object and a class' objectification within the capitalist
labor process.

Second, in order to authorize the empirical investigation he
has conducted, Wright relies on this distinction between pure
"structure-as-such" and its *historical* variation. This investigation necessarily presupposes the "class structure" as an "independent variable" that will be used to "explain" the "dependent variable" (i.e., "class attitude," or "class I.D."). Although
in chapter 2, I demonstrated Wright's failure to construct the

dependent variable "class attitude," I also indicated the anti-Marxist implications this has for a practice of "class consciousness." Wright effectively excluded practical criteria from his definition of consciousness in order to achieve his chapter objective and, most important, to construct this dependent variable.

Just as his social-psychologized "class consciousness" operates as a caused "dependent variable" in an empirical investigation, Wright also attempts to create the necessary causal primacy for his "independent variable" or "class structure." This is the rationale for his claim that "class structure is viewed in one way or another as the 'basic' determinant of the other three elements at least in the sense of setting the limits of possible variation of class formation, class consciousness and class struggle"(ibid.). In "sociologese," this means that class structure causes class effects (e.g. consciousness, formation, and struggle).

Third, Wright practices this "constraint" as the sine qua non of Marxist theory, and given this premise, any relenting on the question of the primacy of class structure (since Wright understands this as the "class in itself") violates this fundamental causal axiom original to Marxist social science.[9] For instance, though Wright argues that his practice of class structure does not peripheralize other dimensions of oppression and domination, he ends up doing so.

> Other mechanisms (race, ethnicity, gender, legal institutions, etc.) operate within the limits established by the class structure, and it could well be the case that the *politically* significant explanations for variations in class formation or consciousness are embedded in these non-class mechanisms rather than in the class structure itself. What is argued, however, is that these non-class mechanisms operate

within limits imposed by the class structure itself. (Ibid., 29.)

Wright's mysterious "class structure itself," abstracted from the historical production of any given concrete racisms, sexisms, or ethnic particularisms, springs to life as the fundamental "empty places" limiting these concrete productions. Of course, Wright's real grounding for demonstrating the subordinate status of these "non-class mechanisms" is to construct them as abstract Weberian social-psychological variables (e.g., race, sex, age, education, attitude). In this way, race, sex, etc., can be practiced as external to class relations and the social relations of the capitalist labor process.

Finally, Wright argues that the "rationale behind this kind of claim [class as "basic determinant"] revolves around the concept of 'class interests' and 'class capacities'" (ibid., 28).

> The argument is basically as follows. Whatever else the concept of "interests" might mean, it surely includes the access to resources necessary to accomplish various kinds of goals or objectives. People certainly have an "objective interest" in increasing their capacity to act. The argument that the class structure imposes the basic limits on class formation, class consciousness and class struggle is essentially a claim that it constitutes the basic mechanism for distributing access to resources in a society, and thus distributing capacities to act. (Ibid.)

Wright's claims on "class structure" are bound up with his argument that "objective interests" are things people "certainly have," and that they are determined by this "basic mechanism." But if objective interests are so objective, why does Wright insist on using quotation marks for their definition?

This indeterminacy was already pointed out in Wright's previous contradictory formulation regarding the objectivity of these "objective interests." On the one hand, Wright claimed that these interests were external to persons: a property of the structure itself. If this were true, however, Wright could not overcome his own historical contingency in order to posit what these objective interests might have been. On the other hand, he argued that the "objective interests" we hold are "deep down inside" the unconscious domains of the psyche. These are universal—belonging to "people in general"—and they consist of an objective preference for "capacity-freedom"—a concept taken from Andrew Levine and corresponding to a liberalist notion of "positive liberty." This objective preference that people in general hold contradicts the first sense that interests are a function of class incumbency. In fact, it amounts to an abstract theory of human nature based in a classical substantialist subject.

Does Wright's claim that "people certainly have an 'objective interest' in increasing their capacity to act" fare any better? I do not think so. Wright's objective interests are imputed by him and are based on his abstract-liberalist practice of value. That capacity-freedom is a necessary premise for the kind of freedom Wright envisions is one thing, but it can by no means be ascribed to a discovery of an already existing internal-psychological or external-structural "objective interest." Furthermore, if the "rationale behind this claim" (i.e., the postulation of real interests and capacities) has no grounding, then what happens to his rationale for a notion of "class in itself"? The failure of one objectivity—"objective interests"—is linked to the failure of the other—"class in itself."

Wright's second conceptual constraint is closely related to the first. "Class structures constitute the essential qualitative lines of social demarcation in the historical trajectories of social change" (ibid., 31). And, as a corollary, "Class struggles are the central mechanisms for moving from one class structure to another. If the map of history is defined by class structures the motor of history is class struggle" (ibid., 32). Whereas the first "constraint" specifies the intrahistorical primacy of "class structure," the second implicates this structure as a transhistorical variable.

The centrality of class relations and class struggle is certainly a position Marxists maintain and provides the historical basis for socialist strategy and revolutionary politics. Within the terms of Wright's argument, however, this "constraint" is plagued by the same problems as Conceptual Constraint 1. There is no basis to suppose that Wright's failure to demonstrate a real causal relationship between independent variable class structure and dependent variables class formation, consciousness, and struggle should be overcome by simply broadening its historical scope. Both constraints 1 and 2 flounder on Wright's inability to bridge the epistemological gap between a consciousness that is conditioned by formation, ideology, and struggles, on the one hand, and a class structure, the objectivity of which resides precisely in its unconditioned and external relation from such individuals and class actors. Furthermore, Wright's failure to authorize a special consciousness in the form of a scientific actor reproduces this relativist dilemma. There is simply no bridge that can traverse the historical formation of class in order to produce an ahistorical knowledge of class structure.

In addition to "theoretical constraints," Wright claims that there are "structural properties of the concept of class" which provide four additional "constraints" on the production of his concept.

> As an abstract concept, the Marxist concept of class is built around four basic structural properties: classes are *relational;* those relations are *antagonistic;* those antagonisms are rooted in *exploitation;* and exploitation is rooted in the social relations of *production.* Each of these properties can be considered additional conceptual constraints imposed on the process of concept formation of concrete class concepts. (Ibid., 34.)

The specification of these four properties of class was early elaborated by Wright (1979b). Rather than critique all four, I focus on one in particular — "antagonisms" being "rooted in *exploitation*" — due to the centrality of this concept in his new concept of class as it is argued in chapter 3 of *Classes*.

This exploitation-based conceptual constraint is argued by Wright in the following way. Defined as "Conceptual Constraint 5" he argues that "the objective basis of these antagonistic interests is exploitation" (Wright 1985b, 36). Wright claims, in defense of his recent acceptance of Roemer's critique of Wright's earlier concept of class, that "while Marx (and certainly many Marxists) sometimes describe class relations in terms of domination and oppression, the most basic determinant of class antagonism is exploitation" (ibid.). "Exploitation," Wright argues,

> must be distinguished from simple inequality. To say that feudal lords exploit serfs is to say more than they are rich and serfs are poor; it is to make the claim that there is a causal relationship between the affluence of the lord and the poverty of the serf. The lord is rich because lords are able, by virtue of their class relation to serfs, to appropriate a surplus produced by the serfs. Because of this causal link between the wellbeing of one class and the deprivation of another, the antagonism between classes defined by these relations has an "objective" character. (Ibid.)

Wright asserts here that exploitation causes (or explains) through some mechanism (defined in terms of a zero-sum relation between persons) a situation whereby one's material loss is caused by another's material gain. The "objectivity" of its character is a claim about its actual existence independent of any possible consciousness reflecting on this "objectivity." Corresponding to this mechanism, and caused by it, are "objective interests."

We would suppose that if exploitation has this "objective" character, then it is a property of the "class in itself." But if this is the case, how is Wright-as-subject authorized to claim what those "objective interests" really are? If Wright fails to establish the "objectivity" of these interests, there is no reason to suppose that the concept of exploitation (designating an equally external "objectivity") should exist.

Wright tackles this problem head on, and once again reveals his repeated failure to distinguish the objective from the merely subjective. Asserting that "this is not the place to discuss the knotty philosophical problems with the concept of 'objective interests,'" (ibid.) Wright offers us a glimpse of the terms of his solution. He claims, "Marx certainly regarded class interests as having an objective status, and the issue here is what it is about those relations that might justify such a claim" (ibid.).

Based on this assumption (one that I also maintain but from a radically different practice of "the objective"), Wright argues,

> The assumption is that people always have an objective interest in their material welfare, where this is defined as the combination of how much they consume and how hard they have to work to get that consumption. There is therefore no assumption that people universally have an objective interest in *increasing* their consumption, but they do have an interest in reducing the toil necessary to obtain whatever level of consumption they desire. An exploitation relation necessarily implies either that some people must toil more so that others can toil less, or that they must consume less at a given level of toil so that others can consume more or both. In either case people universally have an objective interest in not being exploited materially, since in the absence of

exploitation they would toil less and/or consume more. (Ibid.)

Similar to Wright's "constraint" rationale which relied on "real interests" associated with "real structures," Wright for the third time posits a definition of "objective interests." But they are very different from those others that "people in general" possessed. Where do these new "objective interests" come from? The previous critique of Wright's practice of "objective interests" applies equally to this new claim. Wright claims that "the assumption is that people always have an objective interest in their material welfare. . . ." But one may ask, What guarantees this? It is one thing to claim that people must fulfill specific needs in order to practice the kind of world Wright wants to build, but can he really say that people, independent of any human subjectivity, have "objective interests"? No, he cannot. Furthermore, even if they could, which material interests are "objective," and how do we discriminate between rival practices of "the material"? Wright claims that not only do we have an "objective interest" in our material welfare, this welfare is defined as "how much they consume and how hard they have to work to get that consumption."

Even if we grant the so-called objectivity of these interests, there are several problems with Wright's practice of "material welfare." Since Wright is assuming material welfare to be a function of "toil" and "consumption," he has unwittingly (or wittingly) reduced the concept of "objective interests" to accommodate neoclassical marginalist practice. As Wright here specifies these "interests," they apply only to those who consume as toilers, namely, workers. If so, how can "people universally have an objective interest"? How about those who own and control the means of production and labor process? Is their material welfare defined identically with those who do not? If their interests are antagonistic, then this antagonism cannot be expressed as identical interests in relation to social production.

This is one example where Wright's reliance on Roemer's "methodological individualism" has caught up with him. Actual interests produced in and through alienated capitalist production cannot be encompassed by this premise of "methodological individualism" and its grounding in an abstract, egoistic "rational actor."

Second, Wright has failed to justify this latest criteria for arguing the "objectivity" of "material welfare." It appears that perhaps what toiling and consuming have in common, from Wright's vantage point, is a basis for quantification. One can toil more or less; one can consume more or less. In this sense, "the material" is defined in abstraction from what, why, or how one consumes or toils — in short, the *mode* of production. The question of control over the capitalist labor process, for example, is not encompassed in Wright's discussion of what constitutes the "objectivity" of "material interests." Rather than use control over the labor process and concrete social production of human needs as a point of departure, Wright has uncritically assumed an economistic, atomistic, abstract individual (here defined as a consuming toiler) whose needs are defined to suit this humble locale. Arguments regarding functional propensities to toil and consume evoke a bourgeois theorization of a "state of nature," not a Marxist practice of the capitalist labor process. Even more, Wright is not even defining exploitation relations in terms of work as an activity and a social relation. The process of objectifying interests is abandoned in favor of defining exploitation at the level of exchange and circulation relations. To say one has an objective interest in consumption is to presuppose the worker as a mere bearer of income rather than as objective activity making capital possible. Wright has defined exploitation in neoclassicist and Weberian terms by focusing on the exchange of labor for income when in fact the possibility of worker as "bearer" of income already *presupposes* exploitation relations!

Wright also defines "the material" in a way that is at odds with a Marxist practice of "the material." When Marx refers to "the material" conditions of social production, he refers to social practice. "The material" is the historical, and the historical is that which has been actualized and made objective through the labor process (the process of self-objectification.) "The material" also necessarily implies all previous laboring activity. For Marx, "the material" is not and cannot be divorced from the process of materialization, namely, the labor process.

But even if Wright wants to retain this more restrictive definition of the material—"the economic" in the neoclassical and/or Althusserian sense—Wright still fails to make his point. Surely, "the material" qua economic production is constitutive of more than one's "objective interests" in consuming and/or toiling. As pointed out before, this excludes the class of exploiters or what even in mainstream economic terms passes for that ingenious entrepreneurial capitalist agent. Wright clings to quantifiable objects so that his argument (directed at proving the reality of "objective interests") can provide greater grounds for his arguments regarding both the "class in itself" and "real" exploitation mechanisms.

In a last ditch effort, Wright formulates his definition of "material interests." Neither an abstract economistic reductionism nor a non-Marxist practice of "the material" has prevented such an effort. Wright, in defense of the "objectivity" of his definition of "material interests,"claims:

> This formulation obviously side-steps a number of difficult issues, in particular the definitions of material well-being and toil. While in the end there may be an irreducibly subjective element in defining the specific content of each of these, nevertheless I believe there is sufficient continuity of meaning of these terms across contexts that it is reasonable to treat exploitation and the interests structured by exploitation as having an objective status. (Ibid., 60.)

This is one of Wright's most incredible statements. How can something that "in the end" has an "irreducibly subjective element" be postulated as "objective"? Wright apparently turns his back on this "problem" and with theological-like faith asserts, "I believe that there is sufficient continuity of meaning of these terms across contexts." But if interests are "irreducibly subjective," how will Wright posit "sufficient continuity of these terms across contexts"? If statements regarding continuity across contexts must imply the ability to discriminate between difference and sameness, how will Wright overcome his own subjectivity in order to discriminate between this sameness and mere irreducible subjectivity? How can he even begin to know meaning across contexts if he cannot justify it beyond an irreducible subjectivity within each context?

Wright concludes from all of this that "it is reasonable to treat exploitation and the interests structured by exploitation as having an objective status." Along with Wright's desperate invocation of belief and faith (in order to overcome the perils of irreducible subjectivity and hence the loss of "objective" structures and interests) he now concludes by claiming reasonability as if logic had just arrived at its proper destination.

Notes

1. Wright (1985b, 6). Taken from Przeworski's (1977) discussion in "Proletariat into a Class: The Process of Class Formation from Karl Kautsky's The Class Struggle to Recent Controversies." Przeworski cites Kautsky's understanding of capitalist relations of production as "a theory of 'empty places' – places within a social formation dominated by large capitalist production" (p. 347).

2. In a research note, "Class in Itself and Class Against Capital: Karl Marx and His Classifiers," Edward Andrew (1983, 577-584) claims that it is incorrect to associate the notion of class in itself with Marx. Rather, a mistranslation by Kautsky and Bernstein rendered "a class as against capital" into a "class in itself." Andrew cites G.A. Cohen (one of Wright's major acknowledged sources for his structural definition of class) as a strong defender of this false notion.

In any case, the distinction between the categories "in itself" and "for itself" certainly is not original to Marx but goes back within German philosophy at the least to Kant and Hegel, albeit with crucial distinctions between the two over the nature of these distinctions. For Kant, the "thing in itself" designates an ontological category that can be thought (intelligible) but can never be known . Since, according to Kant, all that humans can know is necessarily conditional on sensible intuitions, the phenomenal existence of the "thing in itself" is all we have. The "thing in itself" is by definition unknowable, even though it is logically and necessarily antecedent to phenomena — it is the real (nonsensible or intelligible) object that determines the patterning of phenomena in the realm of sense experience. This seems to correspond much more closely to Wright's notion of "in itself," since, for Wright (as for Kant), this category signifies the "objective" class structure that always remains inaccessible "in itself" save as a theoretical construct grounded in the phenomenal-empirical *representation* of this class in itself.

For Wright, as for mainstream social stratification in general, the real social structure remains logically external to its concept and can at the most be inferred from the "data." We can never really *know* the class structure except through a neo-Kantian-based practice of empirical verification. For Hegel, on the other hand, the categories "in itself" and "for itself" signify the difference between "potentiality" and "actuality." Rather than signify an underlying reality that remains unknowable and innaccessible to the philosopher, the category "in itself" is a claim about the immanent, implicit conditions of existence that have yet to become explicit or actual. This, I think, accords with Marx's practice of this distinction. Of course, Marx first maintained this distinction in a Hegelian manner throughout his earliest writings. Once the metaphysical basis of both Hegelianism and Feuerbachian materialism had been critiqued, however, the "idea" as the "in itself" is replaced with real concrete self-objectification through the capitalist labor process. For Hegel, the category "in itself" is not a statement about a structural condition epistemologically inaccessible to the philosopher; on the contrary, it is a claim about the potentiality for philosophy to make this actual through the objective activity of philosophic labor.

One could argue that Hegel does in fact posit the "in itself" as an unconditioned ahistorical category (as Marx himself once did). Furthermore, this category is actually the ground for self-activity and absolute freedom. This would imply that the "in itself" resides in the telos of an ahistorical Geist logically external from its objectifications within Nature. At the same time, however, Hegel argues that the Notion in itself can only express itself through its externalization in the realm of Nature. That the "in itself" can only become the "in and for itself" through the labor process of speculative reason. It is precisely because the "in itself" is made explicit/actual through the labor of speculative reason that the "in itself" is a category for reflection; that the "in itself" is not only knowable but is made actual through the labor of philosophic speculation.

3. See chapter 1 of this critique for a consideration of the underpinnings of Wright's practice of "science." It is crucial to note that science is always a *historical* formation of practices and that any claim to give science properties that somehow transcend historical production necessarily abstracts from determinant conditions of self-objectification. For example, Wright's appropriation of natural sciences, Althusserianism, "realist" philosophy of science, and sociological methods can hardly be comprehended outside the concrete historical conditions underpinning the social formation of both bourgeois social science as well as certain practices of Marxism. Similarly, the historic-political significance of Althusser's reading of Marx's argument can hardly be understood outside the crisis of Stalinist orthodoxy in France during the mid 1950s and early 1960s.

4. See syllabus to Wright's year-long course taught at Madison, "The Theory and Methodology of Marxist Social Science" (SOC 621-622), 1983- 84, section 8, entitled "Methodological and Epistemological Problems." Wright's "realist" reading of science and Marxism leads to an extended preoccupation with concepts, and so-called concept formation. Wright claims, "The function of concepts is to *penetrate* reality not to *simplify* reality, and to do this concepts must in general not have a one-to-one correspondence to directly observable phenomena. Concepts *attempt* to map real relations, to appropriate the real determinations of social life (determinations which exist objectively independently of the observer) in thought" (p. 87).

5. In the "Preface" to *Classes,* Wright engages in an extended discussion of how various transformations in his life may have affected his Marxist practice. Referring to the "joys of liberated fatherhood," he goes as far as to remark, "I do not know if my theoretical sensibilities have been altered by the wonderful transformation these two little persons have brought to my life." The supposition that asceticism is the correct posture for "truth-seeking" or "theoretical clarity," and that sensuous creative self-objectification impedes such clarity, is a classic theme of Western metaphysics. This stems from the role of knowledge as a *representational* function within classic dualistic epistemology; hence, any clouding of the "mind's mirror" is simultaneously an impediment to such representation. In short, Wright's false dilemma between "theoretical sensibility" and "the joys of liberated fatherhood" has no basis in a Marxist practice. Perhaps a

"dilemma" between revolutionary practice and a more conservative academe is Wright's real concern here.

6. See syllabus to SOC 621-622 (cited in note 4), section 8, "Epistemological and Methodological Problems." See also the "Methodological Introduction" to Wright (1979a) for a good example of Wright's appropriation of "realist" model building. Wright has relied continuously on certain persons for his practice of method. See Wright (1979b) for reliance on Stinchcombe (xxiv, p. 3); reference to Kuhn (p. 18); and use of several mainstream data technicians (xxv). In the same text, Wright uses Althusser (pp.57, 67, 68); Keat and Urry (p. 60). See also pages 228-230 for an extended discussion of the virtues of a scientific Marxism. In Wright (1979a), he makes extensive acknowledgement once again of Stinchcombe's *Constructing Social Theories* (1968), especially "his discussion of the logic of functionalist causation." In addition to Stinchcombe, he uses Althusser/Balibar (p. 17) and "realists" Keat and Urry (p. 12). The admixture of Althusserianism, "realism," and functionalist imagery remains a presence in Wright's continuing argument.

7. Wright's use of "theoretical practice" comes directly from Althusser's categorization of social practice into four subpractices, namely: economic, political, ideological, and theoretical. For this division, see "On the Materialist Dialectic" in Althusser (1969). This privileging of "theoretical practice," though partially renounced in Althusser (1976) — see especially pages 123-124 — continues to be practiced throughout Wright's work. For example, see Wright's "The Status of the Political in the Concept of Class Structure" (1982, 324) for the claim, "Following Althusser, 'practice' can be defined as human activity that transforms some raw material, using specific means of production, into some product." Though Wright alludes to Althusser's "On the Materialist Dialectic" as a reference for this discussion, in this article he himself only explicitly discusses "economic practices," "political practices," and "ideological practices." Nowhere does Wright refer to "theoretical practice" and its "means of production," although for the other practices to make sense, it must be presupposed. See also Wright's "Intellectuals and the Working Class" (1978b), especially pages 14-17, notes 19-22, for Wright's reliance on Althusserian "theoretical practice." Finally, see Wright's syllabus (SOC 621-622, 1983-84) for extensive reliance on Althusser's "On the Materialist Dialectic" as a core source for answering the question "What constitutes 'method' in historical materialism?"

8. For an early reference to the notion that "ideas" are the special products of intellectuals, see "Intellectuals and the Working Class" Wright (1978b, 5) where he claims that "'intellectual' designates a *category of people:* people

whose activity is primarily that of elaborating and disseminating ideas." This article, in general, is a manifesto celebrating the "necessary" relation between those who make history and those who guide it. Consider this statement: "While it is unquestionably true that their ideas were nurtured through contact with the masses, especially in the cause of social struggles, nevertheless it is equally true that the most important contributors to revolutionary theory were not themselves proletarians or peasants. They were intellectuals, and the systematic development of revolutionary theory is impossible to imagine without their contribution" (ibid.).

9. In Wright's syllabus for "The Theory and Methodology of Marxist Social Science" (SOC 621-622, 1983-84), he makes reference to the question ". . . in what sense is Marxism 'materialist'?" Defending the thesis (1983-84, 89) that "economic relations, particularly class relations, define the central limits to the transformation of society as a whole even if within those limits there is no possible reduction of other relations to the economic," Wright then offers his definition of materialism. Wright conflates the material with the economic, and attempts to argue a notion of economic and technological "determination in the last instance." Counterposing "the economic" to the "cultural, ideological and the political," Wright defines the distinctiveness of a Marxist materialism as against its causally pluralist adversaries. For Wright, as for other Althusserian-based Marxist practices, Marxist materialism can be proven to exist if we can establish the causal primacy of the econotechnological over other "subpractices" of social structure.

Chapter 4

False Problems and
New Directions for
Marxist Class Analysis

Erik Olin Wright's failure in *Classes* to produce a coherent, consistently grounded class structure analysis does not mean that Marxism is incapable of constructing such a practice. If my argument is correct to this point, Wright's failure implicates his sociologized and Althusserian grounding and, more recently of course, the neoclassical and liberalist egoism of "rational choice" theory. There is in fact virtually no discussion of Marx's argument regarding the capitalist labor process and the centrality of the process and activity of objectification in the production of class relations. Furthermore, Marx's critique of metaphysically grounded doctrines of knowledge has been replaced with an explicit reliance on a pre-Marxist abstract materialism rooted in the model of natural science.

This final chapter consists of three sets of arguments. The first centers on the implications of Wright's argument (or in this case, lack of one) for his "empirical investigations." I argue that given his particular grounding, Wright's three-chapter "Empirical investigation" in *Classes* (i.e., chapters 5, 6, and 7) is unnecessary and meaningless as a basis for "proving" his particular concept of class structure.

The remainder of this chapter consists of my effort to construct a truer practice of Marxist class analysis. It begins with a radically different practice of the capitalist labor process (i.e., that concrete activity of objectification in and through capitalist commodity production) and, based on this, argues a revolu-

106

tionary alternative to Wright's view of what class structure analysis is all about.

This second part of the chapter consists of an examination of two central Marxist practices and their relation to sociological practices. The revolutionary differences between Marxist and sociological practices of textual objectification provide the first major thrust of this argument. Contrary to Wright's sociologized class analysis, Marx's class analysis as textual objectification — most notably, but not exclusively, those works central to working out and including *Capital* — is based on a model of knowledge production that destroys rather than privileges the grounding for Wright's "class analyst." Beginning with a practice of subjectivity as *objective* activity, Marx's argument regarding the necessity and objectivity of classes is constructed very differently from Wright's. I attempt to demonstrate how such different practices of labor and the labor process ground such radically different practices of class analysis.

The final thrust of my reconstruction of a truer Marxist class analysis, and in fact already implied throughout my critique, is the necessity for practicing the class struggle radically different from that of Wright's abstract class structure analysis. Practicing the class struggle as an academic exercise in sociologized analysis is not Marxist class analysis. Class analysis, if it is to be revolutionizing practice, must be a production that is practiced internal to the process of self-objectification. And, from a Marxist standpoint, this process of self-objectification itself must be practiced internal to the process of class struggle and class formation. Wright's academic construction of abstract definitional boundaries and typologies is not Marxist class analysis. It is one of the usurpations of the name Marxism by a practitioner of Weberian sociology grounded deeply within the abstract materialism of bourgeois liberalist practice. [1]

A Marxist class analysis is the process of making the class struggle. To make class *objective* does not require the total effacement of subjectivity through a special theory of the labor process. Rather, the objectivity of class is the actuality and made-ness of class through the class struggle. To be objective is to *make* class struggle real through your activity as revolutionizing self-objectification.

Wright's argument in *Classes* cannot provide the conditions for, let alone the answer to, the question of class structure. This conclusion follows from Wright's repeated and total failure to ground the knowledge production process in such a way that a real and meaningful knowledge of class structure could be produced. The terms of this repeated failure stem from Wright's abstract, egoistic practice of subjectivity and the equally abstract and externalized practice of objectivity that this abstract labor implies. We have seen that if Wright's principle of subjectivity is used as a grounding for a knowledge of class structure, the most that can be produced is a radically egoistic interpretivist object. Wright's circumscription of a class' conscious being to that of the individual attitude state of an intentionalist "rational actor" may correspond with survey research methods and social psychology, but as a grounding for an epistemology, it is hopelessly subject to the egoism of each "rational actor." There is no reason to believe Wright's argument can escape the now familiar crisis generic to neo-Kantian attempts to generate a true and necessary knowledge of an object whose very "objectivity" resides in an absence of any subjectivity (*read:* meaningful human activity) in its very definition!

My critique of Wright's special (i.e., scientific) theory of the labor process holds the same conclusion for his attempt to attain a knowledge of class structure. Once the uniqueness of Wright's notion of "scientific concepts" is debunked, the boundary between the "conceptual" and the "empirical" is destabilized, and the "objectivity" of Wright's principle "conceptual constraint" is undermined, there is simply no basis by which Wright can even begin to pose the question of "his concept" of class structure. If there is no possible grounding for the production of "concepts" and "knowledges," it is surely the case that Wright's alienated practice denies him the possibility of authorizing his particular concept of class.

In short, Wright's latest attempt to argue a particular concept of class structure simply has no consistently constructed grounding. Instead of being viewed as a crisis of Marxism, however, we should be careful to note that most of the explicit justification for his approach to class analysis relies extensively on non-Marxist philosophies of science and non-Marxist claims with respect to the constitution of a principle of subjectivity.

This lack of grounding has as a further consequence the undermining of Wright's "empirical investigation" and "verification" of his concept of class structure. Though *Classes* includes three chapters (5, 6, and 7) that "prove" Wright's theorization of class corresponds to a real, objective relation and not merely his subjective interpretation of it, nevertheless, such an investigation, as Wright theorizes it, must first be able to ground itself. Once again, the failure to establish a basis for these divisions has led to an inability to pose the terms of his investigation.

Furthermore, Wright's dependent variable "class attitude"— the verification variable within his version of "multivariate Marxism"—was shown to have been constructed at the expense of a Marxist practice of class consciousness and, most important, a Marxist practice of the capitalist labor process. Wright's ontologically individualist "rational actor," while appearing as an improvement over the functional subject of Althusser and Poulantzas, and essential to Wright's practice of sociological verification, undermines Wright's ability to argue beyond radical subjectivism.

Finally, Wright himself unequivocally admits this dependence on mainstream sociological theory and methodology and the non-Marxist assumptions driving his "empirical investigation":

> I will use the term "dependent variable" in the standard statistical sense throughout this discussion,

even though the term usually implies a a rather rigid distinction between "causes" (independent variables) and "effects" (dependent variables). This is at odds with the more "dialectical" view of causation within Marxism within which reciprocal effects between structures and practices is of central concern. (Wright 1985b, 187.)

Given that non-Marxist assumptions govern Wright's practice of the labor process, objectivity, and knowledge production, it is not surprising that Wright explicitly defends non-Marxist practices of "empirical investigation" and "verification" and admits that he is not a Marxist on the fundamental historical questions of what constitutes verifiable truth, meaning, and social causality. Similarly, the terms of Wright's failure to argue class structure analysis must be sought in such non-Marxist practices.

The above quotation, taken even on its own terms, however, fails to articulate the implications it holds for the very questions it raises. For example, it is incorrect for Wright to say that "the term 'dependent variable' usually implies a rather rigid distinction between 'causes' (independent variables) and 'effects' (dependent variables)." This assumption, in fact, is necessary, crucial, and indispensable to the hypothetico-deductive model of natural science that currently undergirds the verificationist-hypothesis testing model of statistical inference used in mainstream Weberian bourgeois sociology. Furthermore, Wright's very conceptualization of causality implies this need to "empirically verify his concept" as *the cause of its effect*. Without such independence, his entire exercise of "empirical investigation" ceases to hold any significance as a mode of "verification."

Though this assumption of analytical-logical independence may be integral to standard social scientific practice Wright correctly claims that it is not rooted in Marxism. Wright writes, in fact, that "this [assumption] is at odds with the more 'dialectical' view of causation within Marxism within which reciprocal effects between structures and practices is of central concern."

If for the moment we accept Wright's false rendition of dialectic,[2] what would be the consequences for his "empirical investigation"? Given the premises driving Wright's practice of 'empirical verification,' the admission or mere hint of "reciprocal effects" between variables "class structure" and "class attitude" is tantamount to denying any special status for Wright's variable.

In conclusion, Wright's sociologized and Althusserian grounding undermines the very possibility of his class structure analysis both as production of a "concept" of "class" and the means of conducting an "empirical investigation" of this "concept." Wright is neither a Marxist on the crucial question of the centrality of the capitalist labor process nor does his class analysis explain anything meaningful regarding the practice of a class' conscious being.

Wright's class structure analysis is an example of what Marx once termed "alienated science thinking itself" within its self-estrangement. There is no amount of "empirical data" that can overcome the fact that Wright's practice is premised in an abstraction from his own as well as others' concrete activity of self-objectification. But once class analysis is deauthorized as an academic exercise, and knowledge is practiced through very different practices of the labor process, the justification for Wright's type of Marxism disappears. It is toward this reconstruction of the labor process and radicalization of Marxist class analysis that I aim to contribute.

Throughout this critique I have discussed Wright's theorization of the labor process and its implication for the very meaning and practice of objectivity. It is now time to turn attention to precisely what I take to be a truer practice of this relation — one that takes class analysis out of the realm of abstract labor and into the heart of the class struggles of alienated labor under capitalist commodity production.

Two modes of a Marxist class analysis are argued. Firstly, drawing on what I consider central to Marx's arguments in the *Economic and Philosophic Manuscripts of 1844,* the *Theses on Feuerbach,* the *Grundrisse,* and *Capital,* I attempt to practice the difference between Marx's practice of textual objectification and that of a non-Marxist sociologism á la Erik Wright. The consideration of Marx's argument concerning the meaning of objectification and the labor process, objectivity, the dialectic, the empirics, historical writing/reading, and the necessity of immanent production, constitute the basis for my argument on Marxist textual objectification.

In the third and final part of this chapter I will move from a consideration of Marxist class analysis as textual objectification to that of class analysis as a non-textual objectification of revolutionizing practice. Here I will attempt to link what I consider a truer practice of the capitalist labor process to the revolutionary activity of its transformation. I will argue that a Marxist class analysis is the practice of class formation and class struggle. The real objectivity of class relations resides not in making abstraction from labor and affixing determinate properties to predictably abstract "structures." Rather, objectivity itself is the objective activity of making class relations real through labor. The strategic-political implications for present-day academic sociologized Marxism of this revolutionary practice of class analysis will then be briefly considered.

Marx's greatest contribution to the history of revolutionizing practice, and on which his entire activity as revolutionary worker was premised, was the practice of human activity itself as *objective* activity. This practice of the labor process provides the basis, not only for his critique of philosophical materialism and/or philosophical practices rooted in extrahistorical authority (e.g., naturalism, transcendental idealism) but also for his critique of political economy. Political economy, as part of that same history, shares the same assumptions endemic in this liberalist bourgeois social formation.

Just as philosophy had failed to grasp the true nature of human labor as the basis for the production of truth and historical practice,[3] political economy was grounded through the same abstract liberalist individualism. Because of this atomistic, "rational actor" individualism, there had been a failure by political economy to pose the real question of the concrete labor process. Political economy *presupposed* rather than *demonstrated* the necessity for the division of labor and capital and grounded its social theory in the standpoints of abstract individuals in exchange relations. Marx points out how this presupposition can neither explain itself nor produce any argument concerning necessary relations in bourgeois society.

> Political economy starts with the fact of private property; it does not explain it to us. It expresses in general, abstract formulas the *material* process through which private property actually passes, and these formulas it then takes for *laws*. It does not *comprehend* these laws, i.e. it does not demonstrate how they arise from the very nature of private property. Political economy throws no light on the cause of the division between labour and capital, and between capital and land. When, for example, it defines the relationship of wages to profit, it takes the interest of the capitalists to be the ultimate cause, i.e. it takes for granted what it is supposed to explain. Similarly, competition comes in everywhere. It is explained from external circumstances. As to how far these external and apparently accidental circumstances are but the expression of a necessary course of development, political economy teaches us nothing. (Marx and Engels 1975, 270-71.)

Well before *Capital,* Marx began to elaborate the labor process grounding his practice of class analysis. Rather than begin with political economy's presupposition of the division of labor and capital (which already implies the capital relation and its premise of a nonowning, commanded working-class), or with Hegel's practice (ultimately reducing the objective activity of labor to pure speculative thinking) Marx characterizes labor as the "rich, living, sensuous, concrete activity of self-objectification" (ibid., 343).

Marx's critique of false practices of the labor process was certainly not restricted to his polemic against so-called "idealism." In fact, the idealist core of abstract, contemplative materialism similarly provided Marx the opportunity to criticize Feuerbach and "all previous materialism" for their failure to practice subjectivity itself as objective activity. In the first thesis in the *Theses on Feuerbach* Marx claims:

> The chief defect of all previous materialism (that of Feuerbach included) is that things, reality, sensuousness are conceived only in the form of the *object, or of contemplation,* but not as *sensuous human activity, practice,* not subjectively. [...] Feuerbach wants sensuous objects, really distinct from conceptual objects, but he does not conceive human activity itself as *objective* activity. In *Das Wesen des Cristenthums,* he therefore regards the theoretical attitude as the only genuinely human attitude, while practice is conceived and defined only in its dirty-Jewish form of appearance. Hence he does not grasp the significance of "revolutionary", of "practical-critical," activity. (Marx and Engels 1976, 3.)

It is only after Marx constructs an argument about labor as objectifying, self-formative activity that he is able to critique the bourgeois particularization of this activity—alienated labor under capitalism. For example, rather than objectification leading to control of the labor process: "Under these [capitalist] economic conditions this realisation of labour appears as *loss of realisation* for the workers; objectification as *loss of the object and bondage to it;* appropriation as *estrangement,* as *alienation"* (Marx and Engels 1975, 272).

Marx's practice of labor as concrete self-objectification allowed him radically to critique bourgeois philosophy and political economy as false practices. As early as 1844, Marx had begun to argue the necessary connection between competitive and monopoly capital, landed nobility and capitalized land. Why was it that political economy could not unravel the secret of "the *money* system"? As Marx points out, as a historical formation political economy could not overcome the abstract, already externalized relations themselves grounded in a similarly abstract Robinsonades eighteenth-century individual.

Because of its grounding in the concrete practice of objectification, Marx's argument concerning the "objectivity" of class relations (or any relations, for that matter) under capitalist commodity production differs in major ways from those of Erik Wright. This radically different practice of "objectivity" and its basis in an alternative practice of subjectivity is explicitly argued once again in the first thesis on Feuerbach. "The chief defect of all previous materialism" Marx claims, "(that of Feuerbach included) is that things, reality, sensuousness, are conceived only in the form of the *object, or of contemplation,* but not as *sensuous human activity, practice,* not subjectively" (Marx and Engels 1976, 3).

Marx is here arguing the distinction between two practices of objectivity. On the one hand, we have the false practice singled out where the object is conceived "only in the form of the *object, or of contemplation."* When the object is conceived merely in the form of contemplation (*Anschauung,* or intuition), Marx is implying that abstraction from the activity of making the object has been made. The object in this sense would be the German *objekt,* designating an external and outside reality. The grounds for such an abstract practice of "objectivity" are themselves an equally abstract and idealist practice of the labor process. Marx explicitly argues this later in this first thesis.

> In *Das Wesen des Cristenthums,* he . . . regards the theoretical attitude as the only genuinely human attitude, while practice is conceived and defined only in its dirty-Jewish form of appearance. Hence he does not grasp the significance of "revolutionary," of "practical-critical," activity. (Ibid.)

It is because Feuerbach and classical materialism more generally begin with a *theoretical* prejudice that the object can appear only "in the form of the *object, or of contemplation.*" There is no other relation of activity implied than that of merely looking upon and contemplating an already constituted externality. This was the essence and arrogance of pre-Marxist materialism in its merely theoretical practice of "objectivity." This is also the basis for Erik Wright's practice of class as a "concept" or "class structure," as an abstract thing with determinate properties.

The second sense of objectivity is captured not in the notion of the *Objekt* but in *Gegenstand.* Instead of "objectivity" conceived abstractly and externally, here it means that "things, reality, sensuousness" are conceived in the form of "*sensuous human activity, practice* . . . subjectively." The practice of making objectivity (the process of self-objectification) is itself objective and therefore has as its product "objectivity." The fact that both the process and product of human activity is here practiced as "objective" led Marx to reject the merely theoretical view of what humans are and do. Humans are not radical theoretical egos sitting in judgment on an already constituted essence; rather, the essence of human life itself is objective activity. The object, then, is merely an objectification of objective human activity in and through previously objectified social relations.

Wright's detached theoretical ego is a constructor of concepts and abides by the ascetic canons of subject-effacing methodological rituals. The self-objectification of objective revolutionizing practice, on the other hand, is a war against this ego and its alienated practice of meaningful human labor. Wright is a twentieth-century Feuerbach, an extension of the very materialism Marx had thoroughly destroyed.

For Marx, therefore, to speak of the "objective conditions" or "objectivity" of historical practice is to argue about the *production* of objectivity. Objectivity implies the actuality and realization of the world as a determinant objectification of labor. The objectivity of the world is a statement about the realization of the world through laboring activity. Given that the object (i.e., objectivity) is in fact an objectification of determinant conditions of laboring activity, there can be no relation of externality vis-á-vis those conditions of laboring activity. "The product of labor," Marx claimed, "is labour which has been embodied in an object, which has become material: it is the *objectification* of labour. Labour's realization is its objectification" (Marx and Engels 1975, 272).

Whereas for Marx, labor itself is objective activity, and objectivity is the product and process of this objective activity, this is clearly not the case for Wright. For Wright, on the contrary, to posit "objectivity" is to *not* make reference to the reality and conditions of determinant objective activity but to demand a relation of externality and independence from such conditions. For example, "objectivity" is conceived as proper to the "class structure in itself" necessarily noncontingent on the particular knowledges of laboring subjects. In direct opposition to Marx's revolutionary practice of the labor process (i.e., labor process as objective activity) it is for Wright the absence of labour in the definition of objectivity which guarantees its "real," "actual," and noncontingent character! The relation between objective activity and objectivity though, can never be one of externality since, both presuppose one another in their very definitions.

An objective being acts objectively, and he would not act objectively if the object did not reside in the very nature of his being. He only creates or posits objects, because he is posited by objects — because at bottom he is *nature*. In the act of positing, therefore, this objective being does not fall from his state of 'pure activity' into a *creating of* the *object;* on the contrary, his *objective* product only confirms his *objective* activity, his activity as an activity of an objective natural being. (Ibid., 336.)

Or, again in reference to alienated objectification, Marx claims:

How could the worker come to face the product of his activity as a stranger, were it not that in the very act of production he was estranging himself from himself? The product is after all the summary of the activity, of production. If then the product of labor is alienation, production itself must be active alienation, the alienation of activity, the activity of alienation. In the estrangement of the object of labour is merely summarised the estrangement, the alienation, in the activity of labour itself. (Ibid., 274.)

Different practices of "objectivity" reflect not merely a debate over words but radically alternative practices of the labor process. Marx, because he begins with the direct relationship of the worker in production, is able to comprehend the object as the objectification of the subject. Wright, on the other hand, begins with an abstract contemplative observer-knower on the one side and an object presupposed as external to and independent of this subject. The only relation Wright theorizes — whether theorizing himself or that abstract "rational actor" of bourgeois neoclassical game theory postulated in his chapter 7 — is a relation of abstract knowing. Consequently, the object appears as a "thing" *(objekt)* external to labor, an objective "class structure as such," with determinant properties and characteristics.

The debate over "objectivity" is also an argument concerning the meaning of purposive activity and necessity. Necessity and those categories dealing with meaningful human activity, for Marx, must be located internal to the determinant conditions of laboring activity in any social formation. Neither a "natural" ruledness nor a supernatural transcendental telos, necessity is a *historical* production—it is a process of creating the objective conditions of social life through objective activity. Marx develops a notion of necessity grounded in the conditions of the capital relation, and hence, argues a radical alternative to Wright's location of purpose as proper to, dependent on, and grounded in what amounts to the abstract, metaphysical proclivities of interacting Cartesian egos.

This point is significant for the following reasons. Wright, in his brief treatment of Lukacs's argument (Wright 1985b, 242-243; See also chapter 2 of this critique) dismisses any notion of "supra-individual" agency by accusing such arguments of being "fundamentally committed to an objective teleology of history" (ibid., 243). Consequently, Wright ends up recognizing the already constituted and presupposed telos of these interacting egoistic "rational actors" and considers indefensible any attempts to produce notions of purposive activity and necessity not premised in "methodological individualism" or "rational choice" theory. The necessity of class relations, in fact, is no longer (if it had ever been) grounded in the necessity of the production relations of capital. Class, as Wright currently argues it, is to be deduced from this initial premise of abstract "methodological individualism" (see chapter 2 of this critique)—whether arguing Roemer's development of this principle or his own modification of it. This involves a rather explicit abandonment of the capitalist labor process and its replacement by the abstract exchange relations of neoclassical bourgeois individualism. As Roemer (1982a) argues, and Wright has apparently endorsed, "it is the differential ownership of productive assets, rather than what happens in the labor process, that is the key determinant of Marxian exploitation" (p. 16).

I have previously argued that Wright's real interest for rejecting the category "supra-individual" resided in his necessity to construct the dependent variable "class attitude" as a measurement for "class consciousness," and given such an interest, Wright jettisoned practices of class consciousness which implicated production relations more generally. The logic of standard empirical sociology and not a production of agency thoroughly within the production relations of capital guided Wright's selection of class consciousness criteria. While Wright (1985b, 280) admits that notions of consciousness, purposiveness, and necessity *can* be located within the production relations of capital as class practices, he nevertheless rejects such a construction.

Finally, a necessary consequence of constituting subjectivity in the terms of a presupposed "rational actor" is to practice "empirical investigation" and its product, "the data," as "objectivities" external to and independent of this subjectivity. For Marx, objectivity—including practices of empirics and theorics—is not external to such activity. Marx verifies-truthifies his argument by locating "the data" and empirics—objectivities produced through and by objective activity—*within, not external to,* the labor process.

Using Marx's practice of objectification and its relation to the practice of objectivity as grounding, it is now time to consider more specifically their implications for a practice of class analysis as textual objectification. Three sets of arguments are made. First, relying on Marx's arguments in the *Grundrisse* and *Capital* I consider in more detail a Marxist practice of empirics. Second, I argue what I take to be a Marxist practice of dialectics, and also, the empirical implications of this dialectic. Finally, I consider both the necessity of immanent construction for revolutionizing practice and the actual relations among the historically abstracted categories of capital, as a basis for such a construction.

Marx's *Capital* is not a rational-logical model of contradiction among mentalistic philosophic concepts; rather, these categories are for Marx themselves historical productions. Just as the commodity labor power has its condition in alienated labor under capitalist commodity production, the conditions for the production of these categories must also be sought in the conditions for the production of alienated objectification.

Marx explicitly acknowledges the historical production of categories practiced by political economy. The commodity-form and abstract labor, for example, presuppose a concrete determinate practice of the labor process. Consider Marx's reference to abstract labor, the very premise of Marx's critique of capital as both value relation and, most important, *social* relation:

> Indifference toward any specific kind of labour presupposes a very developed totality of real kinds of labour, of which no single one is any longer predominant. As a rule, the most general abstractions arise only in the midst of the richest possible concrete development, where one thing appears as common to many, to all. Then it ceases to be thinkable in a particular form alone. On the other side, this abstraction of labour as such is not merely the mental product of a concrete totality of labours. Indifference towards specific labours corresponds to a form of society in which individuals can with ease transfer from one labour to another, and where the specific kind is a matter of chance for them, hence of indifference. Not only the category, labour, but labour in reality has here become the means of creating wealth in general, and has ceased to be

> organically linked with particular individuals in any
> specific form. (Marx 1973, 104.)

The historical process of production—modes of laboring, productive, objective activity—itself grounds the commodity-
form. Unlike the role of concepts in pure logic or Wright's
various "realist" philosophies of science, the commodity-form is
not theorized as a "mental" product. The historicity of the
commodity-form, like that of abstract labor, resides in the
social relations under petty commodity and later capitalist commodity production. Not only does the very possibility of
exchange-value presuppose determinant conditions of laboring
activity, the very possibility of labor itself being produced as a
commodity necessitates historical revolutions in all previous
modes of objectifying activity. In short, the categories of
Capital are not the mentalistic concepts produced by the "rational" abstract man grounding analytical logic and political
economy. Marxism, on the contrary, should be practiced self-
consciously as a revolution against the abstract mentalistic view
of the labor process grounding these practices.

   Just as the commodity-form is not theorized as a merely
mental product, "the facts," or "the data," should not be practiced as externalities that are used to "adjudicate" the concept of
the commodity. Facts are the *product* and *objective* summary
of objective activity. The Latin verb *facere,* from which modern
legal and philosophic notions of facticity are derived, explicitly
grounds facticity as an activity. Meaning *things done* or *things
made,* the factual realm is the realm of human activity and self-
objectification through labor. The practice of *manufacture* (to
be made actual by hand) captures this sense. To investigate the
grounds of facticity, or "the data," then, is in actuality to investigate the self-objectification of labor. If all abstraction is
made from the concrete process of objectification, "the facts" appear as the "phenomena" or "data" of an "objective" (because independent of labor) reality. It is precisely this appearance of

externality that confers upon "the data" the authority to "confirm" or "disconfirm" a "theoretical concept." For Wright, as for bourgeois sociology more generally, facts are practiced as the "phenomena" of the social and not as the objectification of social relations. Once again, the model of natural science turns Marxism into Comte's "social physics."

Armed with a labor-based practice of the categories of political economy and practice of facticity, Marx's argument in *Capital* is a textual objectification (as critique) of the process of alienated objectification under capitalist commodity production.

Having demonstrated that necessary relation—or, more precisely, notions of necessity *given* capitalism's development as a historical formation—is grounded in the objective activity of alienated labor, Marx proceeds to explain necessary connection by focusing on a production of necessity internal to the production of the value relation. At least two necessary conditions must be actualized in order to make the capitalist labor process and the production and realization of surplus value possible: the separation of labor and capital, in other words, that labor itself has been produced as a commodity; and second, that the laws of commodity exchange are operative (i.e., that commodities exchange as equivalents).

The production of labor itself as a commodity (and all social relations implied through this) provides Marx the objective basis from which his investigation of capitalist development was conducted. As early as 1844, even before Marx's later explicit and decisive argument concerning the two-fold nature of labor, he was able to produce an argument about capitalist production relations given this reality of labor as a commodity. "Labour," Marx asserted, "produces not only commodities: it produces itself and the worker as a *commodity*—and this at the same rate at which it produces commodities in general" (Marx and Engels 1975, 272). The rest of this portion of the 1844 *Manuscripts,* posthumously entitled "Estranged Labour," develops these production relations already necessarily implied in the objectification of the subject as a commodity. For Marx at that time, this included a determinant relation of the workers to their products (i.e., objects), labor process, species, nonworkers, and finally, of the relation of nonworkers (from a nonworkers' standpoint) to workers (ibid., 270-282).

Marx's argument so far has been developed as a critique of alienated objectification grounded in determinant, purposive objective activity. The constitution of this activity under conditions of capitalist commodity production also implies practices of necessity and necessary relation that are internal to this unfolding historical practice. It has also been argued that practices of empirical investigation and social research must not postulate verificationist properties that by necessity rely on an extrahistorical or transcendental practice of objectivity for their truth value. Practices of truthification must be grounded in the labor process of historical practitioners who themselves are within this unfolding.

The meaningful practice of a Marxist dialectic provides a second major challenge for Marxists engaged in the practice of class analysis as textual objectification. Before considering the implication of a Marxist dialectic, it is useful to argue briefly what it is *not*. First, contrary to Wright's claim, a Marxist dialectic is not the "more 'dialectical' view of causation within Marxism within which reciprocal effects between structures and practices is of central concern" (Wright 1985b, 187).

As Wright there poses the question of dialectics, it is no more than a bi-directional interrelationism between the two abstract variables "structure" (independent variable) and "practices" (dependent variable). Wright was claiming that if it is possible to think of these two variables reciprocally causing each other, the consequence of this "interactionism" for his own project of correlating "class location" with "class attitude," "class I.D.," etc., would be an undermining of the very basis for his empirical investigation.

The question must be posed, however, where and how Wright produces notions of "structure" and "practice" so that they can be external and merely coincidentally *reunited* through probabilistic statements rooted in probability theory and inferential statistics? Wright's postulation of dialectics here already presupposes two variables that are external to, and independent of, each other in their very definitions and formal properties. In this way, Wright might fear that "class location" (i.e., "class structure") will be confounded out of existence, the implication being that the causal primacy Marxists associate with "class structure" is not statistically significant. I have attempted to show that, in fact, Wright's practice of this abstract "class structure" is grounded in his extremely abstract notions of "practice," or the labor process more generally. Once "practice" is practiced as concrete self-objectification, Wright's "structure" dissolves into the objective activity of the capitalist labor process. Class analysis then is no longer the specifying of typologies but the objectification of revolutionizing practice.

Dialectics is also not the "materialist dialectic" of Althusser or "dialectical materialism" of Soviet party philosophers. In a note to chapter 1 I have outlined what I take to be the basis for the falseness of, and historical grounding for, those practices. As dialectics is there practiced, it is no more than a pre-Marxist and philosophical doctrine that reproduces the traditional relation that had existed between philosophic labor and "the masses."

The precise meaning of "dialectic" and "dialectical contradiction" is, not surprisingly, controversial and fraught with dangers. The practice of a "dialectic" certainly does not begin with Marx, and in order to practice a "Marxist dialectic," it is crucial, in my opinion first to consider the relation of Hegel's dialectic to Kant's, and then, of Marx's to Hegel's.

In Kant's *Critique of Pure Reason,* an entire section is devoted to "Dialectic" and "Transcendental Dialectic," by which Kant means "the critique of dialectical illusion," or a critical treatment of the pure understanding. Kant believed that whereas real knowledge could only be had of phenomenal objects in the realm of sense experience subject to the natural laws of universality and necessity, the faculty of understanding would always be driven to go beyond the confines of these necessary conditions and seek an unconditioned ground outside of all necessary connection in nature. "Dialectic" was understood by Kant as the necessary and inevitable exercise reason would have to perform on itself in order to deflate any attempts by the understanding to go beyond construction of a *canon* (a merely negative condition of all truth) and construct an *organon* (an instrument capable of achieving knowledge of the absolute).

Hegel, in his critique of Kantian dialectic, accepts the terms of Kant's problem, but argues that what for Kant is problematic is in fact the nature of reality itself. In the "Introduction" to Hegel's *Science of Logic* (1969), he claims:

> Kant rated dialectic higher — and this is among his greatest merits — for he freed it from the seeming arbitrariness which it possesses from the standpoint of ordinary thought and exhibited it as a *necessary function* of reason . . . True, Kant's expositions in the antinomies of pure reason, when closely examined, as they will be at length in the course of this work, do not indeed merit any great praise; but the general idea on which he based his expositions and which he vindicated, is the *objectivity of the illusion* and the *necessity of the contradiction* which belongs to the nature of thought determinations: primarily, it is true with the significance that these determinations are applied by reason to *things in themselves;* but their nature is precisely what they are in reason and with reference to what is intrinsic or in itself. (P. 56.)

Hegel, in effect, argued that Kant made the dialectic both objective and necessary. Its objectivity stems from the fact that the mind must engage in this activity, that it is real and actual for the mind's activity. The necessity of the dialectic is something that is less clear from Hegel's passage but one that we can produce. As Charles Taylor (1979, 35) points out, the motor of necessary contradiction in Hegelian dialectic is the contradiction between the purpose, or telos, of Absolute knowledge (essence) and its conditions of existence. Hegel begins with a dualism between Spirit and Nature, Spirit being the realm of the absolute, the in-itself, the realm of subjectivity. Nature, on the other hand, is the alienated and externalized world of Spirit, its otherness estranged from the activity of absolute abstract mind. The contradiction at the heart of Hegelian dialectic, then, is the contradiction that necessarily arises whenever the Absolute objectifies itself in the realm of mere Nature. The end of dialectic, for Hegel, is when Spirit has overcome its estrangement in the realm of Nature and finally realizes Absolute knowledge, thereby ending the activity of the in-itself constantly negating itself (on the road to unconditional knowledge) in the realm of Nature.

Marx's critique of Hegelian dialectic was and remains the key to a practice of Marxist dialectics. I now briefly deal with what I consider the thrust of Marx's critique and then proceed to argue briefly the meaning of dialectic as it is found in *Capital*.[4]

The root of Hegelian dialectic was abstract philosophical labor. Of course, Marx himself, in his earliest works, had accepted the Hegelian standpoint and argued a similar version of dialectic. For example, in his doctoral dissertation, "Difference Between the Democritean and Epicurean Philosophy of Nature," in defense of Epicurus, Marx would claim: "Epicurus objectifies the contradiction in the concept of the atom between essence and its existence" (Marx and Engels 1975a, 58).

In contrast to Democritus, where "there is no realization of the principle itself," Epicurus, by maintaining a notion of active contradictory development, is led to develop "the science of atomistics." Marx would claim:

> The contradiction between existence and essence, between matter and form, which is inherent in the concept of the atom, emerges in the individual atom once it is endowed with qualities. Through the quality the atom is alienated from its concept, but at the same time is perfected in its construction. (Ibid., 61.)

There are countless examples to be found in Marx's earliest works of his radical Hegelianism. Left Hegelianism, however, proved dangerous even within its alienated practice of labor because it led to the conclusive denial of any extrarational claims for authority. To make "God" conditional on "rational cognition" was the end of "God" as steward-savior of the Prussian feudal monarchical state!

Though radical for its time, Marx's ratio-based logic, grounding a critique of the censorship, the Prussian state, etc., would become subject to his own critique. Beginning in 1843-44 and continuing through *The German Ideology,* Part 1, Marx conducted a full-scale assault on the Young Hegelian movement. The grounds for what Marx would call "Hegel's false positivism, or of his merely apparent criticism" had to be exposed. This was one of the central thrusts of the 1844 *Manuscripts.*

Marx begins his critique of Hegel by focusing on the way in which Hegel practices the process of self-objectification. The key to Hegel's system and entire philosophy resides there. Several passages attest to the significance Marx placed on Hegel's alienated practice of the labor process. What were the implications for Hegel's practice of the fact that "the only labour which Hegel knows and recognizes is *abstractly mental* labour"? According to Marx, "Therefore, that which constitutes the *essence* of philosophy — *the alienation of man who knows* himself or *alienated* science *thinking itself*—Hegel grasps as its essence" (Marx and Engels 1975, 333).

Since, for Hegel, "only *mind* is the true essence of man" Hegel's philosophy,

> beginning as it does with logic, with pure *speculative thought,* and ending with *absolute knowledge*— with the self-consciousness, self-comprehending philosophic or absolute (i.e. superhuman) abstract mind is in its entirety nothing but the *display,* the self-objectification, of the *essence* of the philosophic mind, and *the philosophic mind is nothing but the estranged mind of the world thinking within its self-estrangement—comprehending itself abstractly.* (Ibid., 330.)

Given this premise in abstract labor, the object to be overcome, Nature, or better yet, Spirit's alienated objectification in Nature, was no more than an abstraction rooted in Hegel's abstract practice of labor. Marx points out how Hegel's reduction of labor to mental labor transforms the meaning of objectivity to that of a mere relation of knowing.

> The way in which consciousness is, and in which something is for it, is *knowing.* Knowing is its sole act. Something therefore comes to be for consciousness in so far as the latter *knows* this *something.* Knowing is its sole objective relation. (Ibid., 338.)

The history of estrangement for Hegel is thus a *mental* process, and as such the "whole *history of the alienation process* and the whole *process of the retraction* of the alienation is therefore nothing but the *history of the production* of abstract (i.e., absolute) thought—of logical, speculative thought." Marx continues:

The *estrangement,* which therefore forms the real
interest of this alienation and of the transcendence
of this alienation, is the opposition of *in itself* and
for itself, of *consciousness and self-consciousness,*
of *object and subject*—that is to say it is the opposition between abstract thinking and sensuous reality
or real sensuousness within thought itself . . . It is
not the fact [for Hegel] that the human being *objectifies* himself *inhumanly,* in *opposition* to himself,
but the fact that he *objectifies himself* in *distinction*
from and in *opposition* to abstract thinking, that
constitutes the posited essence of the estrangement
and the thing to be superseded. (Ibid., 331.)

The dialectic for Hegel is grounded in the contradiction
arising between abstract mind in the realm of Spirit (in itself)
seeking absolute knowledge, and the object or otherness of
Spirit to be overcome in the realm of Nature. Marx shows how
these divisions themselves are animated by Hegel's philosophic
prejudice in abstract mental labor. Given abstract labor, how is
this estrangement to be overcome? Different views of the meaning
of overcoming estrangement implicate ones practice of labor,
and it is here that Marx's critique of Hegel is so revealing and
devastating. This also shows how political-strategic direction is
already implied through practices of the labor process, a point
that I have stressed over and over vis-á-vis Wright's abstract
sociologism. How, then, is alienation to be overcome? Marx,
arguing this political implication of Hegel's system claims:

The appropriation of man's essential powers, which
have become objects—indeed, alien objects—is thus
in the first place only an *appropriation* occurring in
consciousness, in *pure thought,* i.e. in *abstraction:* it
is the appropriation of these objects as *thoughts* and
as *movements of thought.* Consequently, despite its

thoroughly negative and critical appearance and despite the genuine criticism contained in it, which often anticipates far later development, there is already latent in the *Phanemonologie* as a germ, a potentiality, a secret, the uncritical positivism and the equally uncritical idealism of Hegel's later works. (Ibid., 131-132.)

Here we have the explicit linkage between what Marx terms "the *formal and abstract* conception of man's act of self-genesis or self-objectification" in Hegel and the equally abstract practice of objectivity. One begets the other since, as Marx claimed, there is no relation theorized except that of "knowing," and this "knowing" in turn is based in abstraction from any real determinant practice of self-objectification.

Hegel having posited man as equivalent to self-consciousness, the estranged object—the estranged essential reality of man—is nothing but *consciousness,* the thought of estrangement merely—estrangement's *abstract* and therefore empty and unreal expression, *negation.* The annulment of the alienation is therefore likewise nothing but an abstract, empty annulment of that empty abstraction—the *negation of the negation.* The rich, living, sensuous, concrete activity of self-objectification is therefore reduced to its mere abstraction, absolute negativity—an abstraction which is again fixed as such and thought of as an independent activity—as sheer activity. Because this so-called negativity is nothing but the *abstract, empty* form of the real living act, its content can in consequence be merely a *formal* content begotten by abstraction from all content. (Ibid., 343.)

.

Despite the fact that Hegel's system ends up reproducing the privileged, elitist, and abstract practice of philosophy, Marx was able to realize the revolutionary significance of Hegel's practice of self-objectification through labor. How was this so? Even though "the only labour which Hegel knows and recognizes is *abstractly mental* labor," it was the case that *labor* (however abstract) was Hegel's grounding for the development of absolute knowledge. Spirit only comes to be actual, explicit and for-itself through the labor of speculative thought and hence, objective activity (as thinking) is the basis for the realization of the Absolute.

Marx, as Hegel's most appreciative and revolutionary critic, would claim of Hegel:

> The outstanding achievement of Hegel's *Phenomeno-logie* and of its final outcome, the dialectic of negativity as the moving and generating principle, is thus first that Hegel conceives the self-creation of man as a process, conceives objectification as *loss* of the object, as alienation and as transcendence of this alienation; that he thus grasps the essence of *labour* and comprehends objective man—true, because real man—as the outcome of man's *own labour*. (Ibid., 333.)

Marx would claim, before launching into a critique of the last chapter of Hegel's *Phenomenologie:*

> Let us provisionally say this much in advance: Hegel's standpoint is that of modern political economy. He grasps *labour* as the *essence* of man—as man's essence which stands the test: he sees only the positive, not the negative side of labour. Labour is *man's coming-to-be for himself* within *alienation,* as *alienated* man. (Ibid., 333.)

The practice of Marx's dialectic, as was Hegel's, must be based in the labor process. But Marx's revolutionary critique of Hegel's practice of this self-objectification process breaks with dialectics as a category of philosophy proper. Dialectics, for Marx, is no longer a contradiction "in the nature of thought determinations," as Hegel argued, since *thinking* is not the "essence" of human objective activity. Hegel's abstract laboring ego *thinking* the category of the absolute has been revolutionized by reformulating the process of concrete self-objectification into a *making* of actuality, objectivity, reality, "as the outcome of man's *own labour.*"

Just as dialectical contradiction was internal to the labor process, albeit this process conceived as pure thought thinking itself, a Marxist dialectic must be practiced as internal to the labor process. This labor process must ground itself not in metaphysical absolutes but in historic actuality, in self-objectification through objective activity. The source of contradiction or antithetical (negative) unity cannot reside in the alienated practice of a transcendental Spirit positing, then negating itself, as a condition of attaining Absolute knowledge.

An extremely important question must be answered before we consider the meaning of dialectic for class analysis as textual objectification. If for Hegel, as for Kant before him, the dialectic was set into motion through the contradiction arising between the telos of essence and the conditions of externalized (in this case, naturalized) existence, what sets dialectic in motion after the Hegelian category "in itself" has been overthrown? It is easy to see, given Hegel's standpoint, that dialectical contradiction must be manifest in thought determinations, but since for Marx thinking is no longer the essence of objective activity (labor), how will dialectic be objectified? In other words, can there be a Marxist dialectic based on a thoroughgoing renunciation of any possible metaphysical telos that is at the same time objectified through concrete rather than abstract alienated mental labor? Can we practice contradiction in terms of concrete self-objectification or is contradiction inescapably bound up in abstract philosophic formalism?

I argue that it is possible and that a Marxist practice of textual objectification (e.g., *Capital*) necessitates it. I focus here on *Capital* rather than Marx's other textual objectifications primarily because Marx's entire revolutionizing practice centered around the production of what finally came to be named *Capital*. Marx's analysis of value, the commodity, money, labor and its process, alienated objectification and its conditions of existence, are central themes which ground the entirety of Marx's work. Furthermore, the grounding for a Marxist class analysis must be sought in those social relations which Marx took to be the fundamental bases for the capitalist mode of production, and it is in *Capital* and the works leading to it that these bases are to be found. Finally, though it is certainly the case that Marx's other writings all involve class analysis, and should therefore be considered real practices of the class struggle, they presuppose the arguments produced in *Capital*.

I will consider this question in two parts: (1) What is the basis for a dialectic of labor in capitalist development?; and (2) How is this dialectic of labor developed by Marx in *Capital*? Also, What does it imply for sociological (including "multivariate Marxism" as sociology) practices of causal modelling and empirical verification?

In order for a dialectic to be objectified, a fundamental development must take place, namely, a revolution in laboring activity such that a two-fold division of labor has become objectified. This division, bound up in the commodification of the labor-process, is the division of labor into labor-power as use-value and value. It is this fundamental fact that allows for the possibility of dialectical development. Of course, it is also the case that the division expressed as use-value and exchange-value can be found under conditions where labor-power itself has not yet developed this contradictory existence (e.g. petty commodity production), but for our purposes, this will be subsumed to conditions where it has.

It is crucial to assert, however, even before labor-power itself had been commodified, immanent contradictions stemming from the very metamorphoses of commodities are present. Speaking to the potentiality and future actuality of capitalist crises based in the antithetical unity of the commodity-form itself, Marx would claim:

> To say that these two independent and antithetical acts [M-C and C-M, or buying and selling] have an intrinsic unity, are essentially one, is the same as to say that this intrinsic oneness expresses itself in an external antithesis. If the interval in time between the two complementary phases of the complete metamorphosis of a commodity become too great, if the split between the sale and the purchase become too pronounced, their oneness, asserts itself by producing—a crisis. The antithesis, use-value and value; the contradictions that private labour is bound to manifest itself as direct social labour, that a particularized concrete kind of labour has to pass for abstract human labour; the contradiction between the personification of objects and the representation of persons by things; all these antitheses and contradictions, which are immanent in commodities, assert themselves, and develop their modes of motion, in the antithetical phases of the metamorphoses of the commodity. These modes therefore imply the possibility, and no more than the possibility of crises. The conversion of this mere possibility into a reality is the result of a long series of relations, that, from our present standpoint of simple circulation, have as yet no existence. (Marx 1967, 115.)

Marx has demonstrated that within the contradictory unity of the commodity-form of labor and the value-form of the commodity, a dialectical relation assserts itself. Firstly, use-value becomes a manifestation of its opposite, of value. Secondly, concrete labor becomes a manifestation of its opposite, of abstract human labor. Thirdly, private labor becomes a form of its opposite, labour in a direct social form. In each case, the impossibility of realizing the use-value of a commodity (particularized concrete labor) without at the same time expressing and realizing its value (abstract human labor in a direct social form) presents the possibility of suspending commodity production. This is the case even before wage-labor, and is directly based in the historical commodification process that led to the abolition of directly unified labor as a result of the social division of labor expressed through the commodity-form.

The dialectic of labor begins to express itself in a specifically capitalist form, however, with the creation of the labor-power commodity. It is necessary, therefore, to consider the dialectic in its historically specific instance under conditions of capitalist commodity production. Since under conditions of capitalist commodity production the commodity-form expresses the class relation, class struggles over the imposition of this form must form the basis of a dialectic of labor. Which is to say that the dialectic of labor is, in its basic relational existence, the class struggle.[5]

The first fact of this class struggle was the process of creating the commodity labor-power. The question of whether the commodity-form of work would be imposed on the then non-commodified populations was a bloody struggle, a class struggle. Section eight in volume one of *Capital*, "The So-Called Primitive Accumulation," is the history of that formative stage in the commodification of work, of the creation of the labor-power commodity. It is only after this separation from means of production and subsistence had been achieved that the two-fold nature of labor-power could be objectified.

The next phase of the class struggle was based directly on/in the two-fold nature of the labor-power commodity, namely, the fight over the establishment of a normal working-day. Or as Cleaver (1979) has put it, once the question of *whether* the commodity-form of work would be imposed had been settled, the question of *how much* it would be imposed defined the next phase of class struggles. In order to appreciate the significance and meaning of the working-day, we must more carefully develop the two-fold nature of labor-power. In Marx's first chapter of *Capital,* the two-fold nature of labor-power and the commodity-form objectified by this two-fold labor are analyzed. In fact, according to Marx, this was *the* central basis for comprehending capital as a class relation.[6]

Labor-power has a contradictory existence which can be broken down into the use-value of labor-power on one hand, and the value of labor-power on the other. Each of these poles in turn can be analyzed in terms of their qualitative and quantitative aspects. Let us develop these relations further. The use-value of labor-power considered in its qualitative aspect is useful labor, or, the actual, concrete, specific attributes of self-objectification. The quantitative aspect of labor-power as use-value is the actual labor time, or, the actual labor time of concrete labor. In both the qualitative and quantitative senses, then, the use-value of labor-power is the specific concrete activity of living labor as measured in time. In short, the use-value of labor-power is labor.

If we consider the labor-power commodity from the standpoint of its existence as value, however, we begin to see the grounds for the class relation and class struggles over/through/as that relation. The qualitative aspect of labor-power as value, according to Marx, is its substance as abstract labor. Abstract labor, or what I term the capacity for alienated objectification in general, is the qualitative aspect of labor-power as value. Abstract labor, as noted in the earlier quote from the *Grundrisse,* is not the abstract concept of labor, but the actuality of labor under conditions of commodification. As Marx claims, "This definition of value . . . is only the most abstract form of bourgeois wealth. It already presupposes 1. the destruction of natural communism (in India etc.); 2. the destruction of all undeveloped, pre-bourgeois modes of production which are not governed in their totality by exchange. Although it is an abstraction, it is an historical abstraction which can only be assumed on the basis of a particular economic development of society."[7] The quantitative aspect of labor-power as value is the measure of this abstract labor, or more familiarly, socially necessary labor time. Socially necessary labor time is that time necessary to create the conditions of existence (i.e. the means of subsistence for the labor-power commodity) that enable the use-value of labor-power to be consumed (actual labor time).

Returning to our example of the working-day, we can see that once labor-power has been commodified in this two-fold way, the source of surplus-value will be the difference between the use-value of labor-power (i.e. the consumption by capital of labor-power's life activity or labor) and its value (i.e. the socially necessary labor time required to reproduce the value of labor-power). As a purchaser of the commodity labor-power and therefore entitled to the use-value of its commodity, capital consumes actual labor time while only paying for socially necessary labor time. Absolute surplus-value, then, is the strategy that capital adopts in order to maximize the use-value of labor-power (labor) by expanding that part of the day which exceeds socially necessary labor time.

The commodification of living labor and its control by another class grounds the dialectic of labor. It is only because the use-value of labor-power belongs to another class that a struggle exists over how to extract the maximum possible labor time from labor-power. This in turn presupposes the commodification of all means of production and means of subsistence.

Once the establishment of the normal working day had been achieved and capital's strategy of absolute surplus-value had been confronted, capital was forced to adopt new strategies in order to extract/control labor's use-value. The class struggle over the use-value of labor-power shifted to the strategy of relative surplus-value. It is here that the class struggle which grounds both the actuality of labor-power's alienation and the possibilities of abolishing that alienated objectification are to be discerned.

The maximization of actual labor time, given the establishment of the normal working-day, can only be achieved by capital in a way that undermines the possibility of capital's rule. This is the basic dialectic that Marx presents in his chapters on relative surplus-value. The essence of the problem for capital is this; How to increase the actual use-value of labor-power (labor) once actual labor-time has been limited. The strategy that capital is forced to adopt, given the contradictory existence of labor-power as a source of surplus-value for capital, is to decrease socially necessary labor time as a proportion of actual labor time. But this is precisely the problem. Only living labor can be a source of labor's use-value for capital, but the condition for expanding this use of living labor's time is the reduction of socially necessary labor. This cannot be done without replacing living labor with dead labor. In other words, in order to increase the use-value of labor, capital must replace living labor with dead and thereby kill the goose that lays the golden eggs! Only on condition of increasing the productivity of labor-power (reducing the value of labor-power) can capital extract surplus-value, but it is precisely this same process that forces capital to undermine its very condition of class rule, namely, control over the labor process of living labor.

Throughout the whole of *Capital* Marx illustrates this dialectic of labor while at the same time grounding it thoroughly in and through class struggles. What is most outstanding is the two-sided nature of all the categories of capital and how a two-sided meaning emerges from the class struggle. In the case of the strategy of relative surplus-value, for example, Marx shows how "the application of machinery to the production of relative surplus-value implies a contradiction which is immanent in it, since of the two factors of the surplus-value created by a given amount of capital, one, the rate of surplus-value, cannot be increased, except by diminishing the other, the number of workmen" (Marx 1967, 384). Of course, it is this necessary replacement of living labor by dead that forces capital to transform machinery into a means for infinitely expanding the working-day and increasing its intensity. Marx continues, "Hence, the economic paradox, that the most powerful instrument for shortening labour-time, becomes the most unfailing means for placing every moment of the labourer's time and that of his family, at the disposal of the capitalist for the purpose of expanding the value of his capital" (ibid.).

The basis for a Marxist dialectic resides in the fact that the self-objectification of labor-power as both use-value and value creates *simultaneously* the basis for transforming the self-objectification of labor as this two-fold existence. The very process and success of labor-power as creator of use-value (its determinant, specific creative objectification) conflicts with and undermines the value of labor-power (labor-power as the capacity for and activity of alienated objectification). I have briefly posited a few of the dialectical determinations of the class struggle in order to illustrate that firstly, the dialectic is the class struggle and its terms are the class relation, and secondly, that a Marxist class analysis must be grounded in this class struggle.

Marx has succeeded in displacing the basis of dialectic from the metaphysically practiced contradiction between essence and existence in Hegelian and Kantian philosophy to the realm of concrete self-objectification. The abstractly universal telos of an absolute author was replaced with the historically specific telos of a determinant mode of self-objectification.

What, then, are the implications of this practice of dialectic for the practice of class analysis as textual objectification? Through this practice we can rule out a number of false practices that ground dialectic not in the process of self-objectification but in complete abstraction from this process.

First, Marx's practice of contradiction is not grounded in logic. It is not the abstract, metaphysically animated negation of an ahistorical telos by its externalized-naturalized existence. The categories bearing this contradiction are the historical abstractions of the class struggle, themselves grounded in the concrete self-objectification of a specific commodity: labor-power. That laboring activity is expressed as both production of use-value and value is itself conditioned on the very possibility that labor-power can be bought and sold as a commodity. The real object/subject of Marx's class analysis is the historical over-throwing of capitalist commodity production and, most crucially, the abolition of living labor's commodification. Therefore, instead of textual objectification being removed from the domain of self-objectification, *Capital* should be self-consciously practiced as embodying the real categories of the class struggle and hence a weapon in the hands of the working class. It is a means for deciphering the class relations of capital from the standpoint of living labor in order to revolutionize them.

Secondly, as noted earlier, the elitist distancing from class struggle that Wright's version of "materialist dialectic" ("DIAMAT") implies must be rejected. His practice of dialectic does not refer to the process of labor's self-objectification at all nor to any specific self-activity of the working class. It is, for him, a philosophy of science authorizing a pre-Marxist and metaphysical grounding for the process of knowledge production. Wright's use of this dialectic, in fact, is used for constructing "the concept of class" instead of practicing the class struggle. It is an elitist practice that reproduces the grounding for sociologized Marxism, as well as Marxisms that reproduce a "necessary" relation between the objective activity of the working class and the objective activity of their concept constructors.

Finally, a dialectic of labor undermines the basis of any dialectic that alleges to be *between* two things, whether these are two "variables" ("practice" and "structure" for Wright) or are theorized as two separate spheres of "social structure" (e.g., "base" and "superstructure"). The conjunction "and" in both cases appears harmless but in fact represents a total failure to locate the dialectic as internal to the self-objectification of labor. It is precisely the abstraction made from this self-activity that allows the "theorist" to construct these two "separate" realms of society. In most cases, dialectic is used as a synonym for interactionism or dynamism, which in itself, does not seem problematic, but an attempt is made to recreate an elitist distance between the activity of thinking-thought on the one hand, and the rest of objective activity on the other. Dialectic is brought in here as a word to signify that the "theorist" is and must be in a dynamic relation to his/her object of theorization. In short, similar to "DIAMAT," this dialectic is also used to ground the distance between two spheres, one of which is superior to society.

Erik Wright's sociologized class analysis relies on both of the above practices of a false dialectic. His class analysis as textual objectification is dialectical only in the sense that he relies on the academic distance "materialist dialectic" introduces and gives lip service to the "interaction" that may exist between his ' two variables "structure" and "practice." Dialectic is there used as a doctrinaire scientific grounding and does not apply, therefore, to either the self-objectification of labor nor the very activity of textual objectification. Dialectic is internal to the labor process under capitalist commodity production. The grounds for Marx's dialectic are to be sought in the purposive objectifications occurring through and in production relations, not in the external, formalized criteria for variable construction in Weberian sociology.

A Marxist practice of dialectics radically departs from standard notions of causality that ground Wright's practice of "multivariate Marxism" or, sociological practice more generally. Sociological practices of causality imply a relation of externality and primacy for a determining agent (e.g. an independent variable) and a relation of contingency for the determined effect (e.g. a dependent variable). The question remains, however, how such an independent, externalized causal agent can be established without lapsing into idealism. The search for antecedent conditions of antecedent conditions is in actuality the search for an origin that itself is non-relational, absolute, and historically unconditioned.

Unlike the Cartesian causality grounding practices of determination in sociology or sociologized Marxism, however, *Capital* is not a representational objectification, a picture book depicting the development of capitalism from its origins to the present. It is the unfolding of a dialectic of labor, and this unfolding itself is grounded directly in the process of self-objectification in the capitalist labor process. Let us consider the implication of this for what are usually referred to as textually objectified "empirical investigations."

Empirical investigation, as was pointed out earlier in this chapter, in order to be true, must not abstract from the conditions of self-objectification. Earlier I discussed this in relation to the authority Wright tries to derive from "the data" due to their apparent externality from his process of "concept formation." I argued that contrary to Wright's neo-Kantian sociologism, Marxists must not rely on making such abstraction from their own labor processes, and in fact, empirics practiced in this way cannot truthify-verify the objectivity of class at all. This does not imply the specter of rationalism, since for Marx, unlike pre-Marxist philosophical practice, objectivity is not produced by the intellect in its abstraction from the world. Objectivity is the objectification of objective activity. And the essence of objective activity is not the mind's abstract existence but the concrete self-objectification of labor within and through conditions of previously objectified labor.

Capital, based within a historically specific practice of objective activity, provides an example of Marx's revolutionary practice of the empirics. By locating an empirics internal to the dialectic of labor, Marx was able to objectify the actual content of class relations as they developed through the class struggle.

Marx's deployment of social research and "empirical data" does precisely that. Thousands of pages of data (e.g. Engels's Blue Books, British factory inspectors, physicians, and bourgeois statisticians) were used by Marx to illustrate the internality of this dialectical self-objectification of labor-power. Whether it is the necessity of the struggle over the length of the working-day (self-objectification as class struggles over absolute surplus-value) or relations of handicraft production, manufacture, and machinofacture (self-objectification as class struggles over relative surplus-value), those empirics can never be abstracted from the process of labor's self-objectification.

Marx's use of social research and his practice of empirical investigation is not used to confirm or disconfirm an abstract definition of capital, or class, or any kind of "independent variable" or "concept" in a sociological sense. The meaning of machinofacture vis-á-vis manufacture cannot be demonstrated through multiple regression equations and statistical inference procedures. Only by grounding the production of objects within relations of self-objectification (capital as social relation) was Marx able to "explain" the meaning and necessity of machinery. This necessity is and was linked to the production of surplus-value, without which machinery takes on a character of mere "thingness," of randomness.

A Marxist class analysis as textual objectification not only has to reject a false dialectics and empirics, but must: (1) self-consciously practice itself as an immanent rather than transcendent presentation and, (2) ground itself in the actual relations of capital's historical abstractions and not in their relation to an origin. These two practices will be respectively considered.

The textual objectification of class analysis must always be practiced as an immanent production. Marx's critique of capitalism involved a starting-point for practice which was crucial for any attempts at revolutionary historical transformation, namely, Marx himself, qua revolutionary worker, had to remain *thoroughly within and an integral part of* the history he was critiquing.

One central feature of this historical relation is the distinction within a process of self-objectification between a mode of investigation and the mode of presentation. This distinction must be practiced in the construction of any — textual or nontextual — mode of class analysis. What precisely does Marx mean by this distinction? Let's consider a crucial passage from the "Afterword" to the second German edition of *Capital:*

> Of course the method of presentation must differ in form from that of inquiry. The latter has to appropriate the material in detail, to analyze its different forms of development, to trace out their inner connexion. Only after this work is done, can the actual movement be adequately described. If this is done successfully, if the life of the subject-matter is ideally reflected as in a mirror, then it may appear as if we had before us a mere a priori construction. (Marx 1967, 19.)

The method of inquiry Marx here makes reference to is both mode of self-objectification and an objectification of certain production relations. Marx's activity of producing *Capital* as self-objectification of inquiry implies a determinate product. Copious notebooks were compiled, thousands of texts were read, and year after year was spent producing — within these relations—Marx's self-objectification as investigation of the conditions and possibility of capitalism.

Marx's mode of self-objectification within this investigative relation determined the form this work would take. If the object is the objectification of the subject, as I have argued, the determinate conditions of Marx's labor shaped the very possibility and meaning of his work during that mode of laboring activity. Consequently, appropriating materials, analyzing forms and inner connections, etc., cannot be transported willy-nilly out of that relation of laboring activity. There is no reason to believe that others not engaged in that process of self-objectification should be able to comprehend the summary of that process.

The method of presentation, on the other hand, while also a determinate productive activity, must be constructed differently from the mode of inquiry. The self-objectification of labor as mode of presentation is based on the fact that previously objectified social relations will be the point of departure for those reading-writing the meaning of this self-objectification. In other words, in order self-consciously to practice a mode of presentation, one must necessarily begin with accepted, more or less taken for granted assumptions and practices of a determinate social formation. Given that the historical self-objectification of the reader-writer is also crucial to either producing or undermining the possibility of critique, there is no other choice, unless one chooses to engage in a transcendentalism that eschews any historical basis for self-objectification. The previous conditions of laboring activity must themselves provide the point of departure for any critique which is fundamental. The necessity of beginning with previously objectified social relations is precisely what separates historical from utopian practice.

Before one can argue and defend a truer critical practice, it is necessary historically to deconstruct existing practices. Consider Marx's self-conscious practice of this necessity in two examples, one from the 1844 *Manuscripts* and a second from *Capital*.

> We have proceeded from the premises of political
> economy. We have accepted its language and its
> laws. We presupposed private property, the separa-
> tion of labour, capital and land, and of wages, pro-
> fit of capital and rent of land—likewise division of
> labour, competition, the concept of exchange-value,
> etc. On the basis of political economy itself, in its
> own words, we have shown that the worker sinks to
> the level of a commodity and becomes indeed the
> most wretched of commodities. (Marx and Engels
> 1975, 270.)

The necessity of engaging political economy within its own
terms and grounding as a condition for producing a revolutionary
alternative to it is nowhere clearer than in that passage. Marx
demonstrated, *given the terms of political economy itself,* that it
could not account for the very possibility of capitalist production. It could not comprehend the necessity of the "wretched
commodity" labor power in its own language and laws. Not only
did Marx have to be thoroughly within the political economist's
system in order to critique their most basic premises, this was a
precondition for any alternative argument Marx was to construct. The following pages in that manuscript are such an alternative.

Capital is also produced self-consciously as a method of
presentation. Parts 1 and 2 of volume 1, for example, develop in
far greater complexity and detail the argument Marx was
already making in the 1844 *Manuscripts.* Proceeding from the
very laws of commodity exchange—namely, that commodities
exchange as equivalents—Marx was able to demonstrate the impossibility of accounting for Ṁ in the general formula M-C-Ṁ.
The necessity of chapter 6, "The Buying and Selling of Labour-
Power," was grounded in Marx's demonstration in chapter 5
"Contradictions in the General Formula of Capital" that the
commodity labour power was the necessary condition for capital.

Moreover, without working through the laws and conditions of political economy as they presented themselves, Marx's presentation might as well of fell on deaf ears.

Not only *Capital* in general, but every discussion within it was constructed as a presentation. Marx had to work through the false consciousness of this bourgeois social formation and each category within it. For example, consider Marx's discussion of the commodity-form. He begins with a consideration of commodities as they "appear," as they "present themselves": "A commodity is, in the first place, an object outside us, a thing that by its properties satisfies human wants of some sort or another" (Marx 1967, 35).

This, of course, is the appearance of commodities as they present themselves in the realm of exchange relations. This is the dominant practice of commodities as "things" with "intrinsic properties" that satisfy. Clearly Marx was aware of the falseness of this statement. Yet this apparent reality had to be taken seriously as a point of departure. Of course Marx finishes chapter 1 with a discussion of the very conditions producing this appearance of "thingness" and externality vis-á-vis commodities. The "fetishism" that attaches itself to commodities is grounded in the very conditions of laboring activity whereby the socialized activity of self-objectification is lost sight of. Objectivity is no longer grounded in social relations among people but in the intrinsic, extrahistorical qualities of the things themselves (ibid., 71-83).

The necessity of immanent rather than transcendent methods of presentation is linked to another question, namely, traditional sociological practices of "history." How does Marx self-consciously practice "the order of things," questions of "pastness," and the meaning of history itself?

Marx's practice of historical unfolding, as may be evident by now, is not a linear, sequential temporality mirroring capitalism from its "origins" to the present moment. The temporality-spatiality of capital, for Marx, is internal to the process of self-objectification and therefore must be grounded there. Whereas Wright's model of empirical investigation relies on assumptions of variable independence, primary causality and correlation of phenomena within Cartesian time-space, Marx grounds his investigation self-consciously as a mode of presenting the dialectic of labor. Marx historicizes the production of time-space in the labor process, while Wright ahistorices time-space relations as a condition of isolating independent cause and dependent effect similar to experimental methods in natural science. These different practices of temporality implicate not just practices of empirical investigation but, most important, the very meaning of history as a production of "pastness."

How does Marx develop his argument concerning the "history" of capitalism's development? How does his practice differ from conventional notions of history as representing "what really happened" independent of the here-and-now acts of cultural, historical producers?

An argument concerning the history of capitalism should address at least two important considerations. First, an argument concerning the conditions of historical development must simultaneously and self-consciously be practiced as a critique of the conditions of capital as a mode of production. Second, the elaboration of the conditions of capital's development must proceed from their decisiveness within capital, not in conventional accounts of temporal history.

Marx indicates in the *Grundrisse* that a critique of capital is simultaneously a rewriting of history. This rewriting of history is and must be consciously practiced as such, and given this, the traditional "externality" accorded to historical data, must be radically dispensed with. In a key passage Marx claims:

> The so-called historical presentation of development is founded, as a rule, on the fact that the latest form regards the previous ones as steps leading up to

itself, and, since it is only rarely and under quite specific conditions able to criticize itself. . . it always conceives them onesidedly. (Ibid., 106.)

Marx continues, "Likewise, bourgeois economics arrived at an understanding of feudal, ancient, oriental economics only after the self-criticism of bourgeois society had begun" (ibid.).

Locating the production of "past history" as a production of the present critique of bourgeois society radicalizes contemporary sociologized Marxist practices of history. As Marx here asserts, the production of the present is simultaneously a reconstruction, a rewriting of historical development. This does not necessarily imply that all accounts of history have equal validity with respect to the goal of a Marxist practice. Truer accounts must ground themselves in the concrete process of self-objectification, the very process and historical mode of self-objectification. False histories, then, fail to critique or even locate these necessary conditions grounding determinant objective activity. One thing is sure. Given that trueness is grounded in an argument concerning the very possibility and necessity of objective activity and *not* in an assertion about some real "external" historical datum being brought to bear on this or that hypothesis, Marx's practice of empirical investigation radically challenges a major premise of Wright's sociologized Marxism. Proving the neccessity and reality of capital or "class structure" cannot be accomplished by dredging up some "really there" historical data that somehow lie outside of—transcend—the trueness or falseness of an immanent critique of capital. History writing-reading is no longer an attempt at temporal representation from the origin. It is the self-conscious revolutionary making of history as a concrete self-objectification of labor.

The second point, that succession of the categories must be grounded in their decisiveness for capital, not in conventional, linear temporality, is equally crucial to Marx's practice of empirical investigation. I have mostly covered this point by arguing earlier over the necessity of practicing data as a category internal to the unfolding of immanent contradiction in capital.

An additional claim for this necessity can be found in the *Grundrisse:*

> It would therefore be unfeasible and wrong to let the economic categories follow one another in the same sequence as that in which they were historically decisive. Their sequence is determined, rather, by their relation to one another in modern bourgeois society, which is precisely the opposite of that which seems to be their natural order or which corresponds to historical development. The point is not the historic position of the economic relations in the succession of different forms of society. Even less is it their sequence "in the idea" (Proudhon) (a muddy notion of historic movement). Rather, their order within modern bourgeois society. (Ibid., 107-108.)

Marx's production of that "order within modern bourgeois society" is rooted similar to his argument on "past history" in his practice of a dialectic of labor. The question of order is really a question of *how* capitalism is made, the mode of self-objectification. For Marx, the question of the meaning of history has been transformed into the question of how history is made. The objectivity of history must be located in and through the objective activity of labor. With this question, the meaning of history itself has been revolutionized. Or, as Marx once put it:

> We have already gone a long way to the solution of this problem by *transforming* the question of the *origin of private property* into the question of the relation of *alienated labour* to the course of humanity's development. For when one speaks of *private property,* one thinks of dealing with something external

to man. When one speaks of labour, one is directly
dealing with man himself. This new formulation of
the question already contains its solution. (Marx
and Engels 1975, 281.)

Textual objectification remained a central feature of Marx's
objective activity but certainly was not his sole objective activity.
These concluding remarks deal with what I take to be the
outlines of a revolutionary alternative to present sociologized
class analysis, one firmly based within a Marxist practice of
knowledge production.

The grounds for Marxism as revolutionizing objective activity
are to be sought in the fundamental critique Marx makes of the
alienated practices of philosophy and political economy. It is
unsurprising that neo-Kantian-grounded sociologized Marxism
(e.g., Erik Olin Wright) has never, to my knowledge, engaged
this part of Marx's argument. In the case of Wright, this part of
Marx's argument was effectively "read out" through the
academic sociological reception of Althusser's reading of Marx.
Marx's alternative practice of knowledge production was
cavalierly dismissed as part of "humanism" or relegated to the
concerns of philosophy. Nevertheless, the revolutionary
strategic-political implication of Marx's practice of knowledge
production must lead us beyond present sociologized Marxism.

Marxism, as a truer practice of the labor process (the process
of self-objectification), gains its revolutionary significance
from overthrowing the liberalist social formation. In other
words, the meaning of Marxism is based on the revolutionary
alternative it poses to the very way we practice the meaning of
life activity. How is the social made? What is the relation of
self-objectification, and what significance does it hold for the
production of meaning and objectivity? Marxism is not a subset
of sociological theory seeking to replace one hypothetical
abstraction with another. Marxism calls into question the very

meaning of the "theoretical," "knowledge," and "objectivity," instead of uncritically assuming them as point of departure.

Previous to Marx's critique, and continuing in post-Kantian alternatives to Marxism ever since, philosophical grounding has been sought in an intellectual labor process. Understanding, or reason (seated in the mind) provided the basis from which knowledge could be produced regarding meaning and the objectivity of the world. The activity of philosophic labor consisted of producing mental representations of this world whose very objectivity was derived from being outside and external to mere thinking. On one side stood the grounding for philosophic activity — the abstract, thinking mind — and on the other, an external reality — in short, on one side "the subject" and the other "the object."

The question is, How does a truer Marxism revolutionize this philosophic practice of labor so that it is exposed for what it is — an example of alienated self-objectification — and place it on a real, actual foundation? I have covered some of this terrain in the earlier discussion of Kantian, Hegelian, and Marxist dialectic, but now go into more detail.

Hegel, as Marx points out in his work from the 1844 *Manuscripts* to *Capital,* even in his alienation, had located the process of knowledge production within the process of self-objectification. Hegel understood the necessity of truth-making as an activity, as process of development. Hegel provided, though retaining the indefensible prejudice of philosophy, one of the possible futures for post-Kantian philosophy.

Contrary to the Kantian system and its post- and neo-Kantian adherents, Hegel argued that absolute knowledge of reality could be had. The unwarranted restriction of reason to phenomenal knowledge, Hegel would argue, was based on Kant's failure fully to acknowledge the activity of reason in the formation of objectivity. The mind itself is objective activity, and as such the reality and actuality of the objective world should never be beyond the scope of reason. The fact that the mind itself posits the absolute as a category for reflection means that absolute knowledge can be had of reality. Of course, Hegel's grounding in abstract mental labor led him to characterize reality solely as the mind's self-objectification, and hence objectivity was practiced in abstraction from the broader process of self-objectification. In short, Hegel critiqued Kant's philosophy from the standpoint of reason's objective activity as a process of self-development. The world as objectivity for Hegel consisted in successive modes of reason's self-formation (*Bildungs*). History was the process of mind's self-development — thus, an *educational* history — through the mental labor-process of speculative dialectic.

It is not hard to see how Hegel's system could and did authorize left-wing, centrist, and right-wing practices. In the case of the Young or Left Hegelians, Hegel's argument issued in rationalist criticism of Prussian Christian monarchical authority and led to atheism and political radicalism. Marx's earliest writings are a Young Hegelian manifesto against these unwarranted and self-serving authoritarian strictures placed in the way of Spirit's rational realization in and through rational freedom and the modern nation-state. On the other hand, the Hegelian system could and did lead to intellectual arrogance and a reactionary politics, both of which are already implied in the privileged locus abstract reason occupies in Hegel's argument.

While Hegel places knowledge in the realm of mind's self-objectification, the entire Hegelian system presupposes the privileged philosopher (Hegel as phenomenological observer) who himself is merely witness to this unfolding dialectic. This intellectual privileging was the topic of Marx's most fiery polemics directed against the Young Hegelian school. *The Holy Family, Theses on Feuerbach,* and *The German Ideology,* for example, fundamentally assault that most precious premise of Hegelianism and Feuerbach's idealist and abstract materialism, namely, the subject as abstract mental labor.

How did Marx both radically critique Hegel and at the same time appreciate this most significant practitioner of post-

Kantian philosophy? Marx's revolution against Hegel was based in his displacement of the Hegelian labor process in favor of Marx's truer practice. The process of self-objectification was not, as Hegel argued, grounded in the objective activity of mind; rather, objective activity was based in the transformative labor of a total self-objectification. It was not merely a mental object but a practical, revolutionary, historical object grounded in objective relations of self-objectification. Hegel had privileged the standpoint and grounding of philosophy (as did all Marx's predecessors), importing along with it its elitist, reactionary, and false practice of the labor process. The very practices of self-objectification, objective activity, and objectivity were transformed from the realm of speculative mentalistic labor to the realm of concrete self-objectification.. The abstract labor of mind was transformed into "productive, life activity itself."

So it is not really the case (despite Marx's own statements, which were bound up with the polemic against German idealist philosophy) that Marx turned Hegel (who was standing on his head) back onto his feet. Hegel had always had two feet on the ground (just as present-day sociologized Marxism does) but abstracted from real, actual transformative life activity (i.e., labor). Marx's revolution against Hegel did not consist in a turning right-side-up but in remaking the very meaning of labor itself; in making concrete, what was in Hegel, alienated abstraction.

While Marx's critique of Hegelian philosophy is mostly alien to the present debates in sociologized Marxism, much credence is given to Marx's *Theses on Feuerbach,*[8] especially the eleventh thesis. The *Theses* are considered by many to be an extraordinary distillation of revolutionary spirit and enthusiasm. But the *Theses* can also be used as a revolutionary weapon against present-day Wrightian sociologized Marxist class analysis. It can be argued, in fact, that they provide the central features of Marx's revolution against the abstract labor grounding academic class analysis.

Marx's *Theses on Feuerbach* provide a fundamental alternative to present practices of theory, knowledge production, objectivity, and the very meaning of subjectivity. Their significance goes well beyond the philosophical debates of the 1840s to engage the very foundations of Wright's sociologized Marxism. What exactly was/is at issue here?

The *Theses* present two fundamentally different practices of labor that lead to radically different strategic-political conclusions. The eleventh thesis — "The philosophers have only *interpreted* the world, in various ways; the point is to *change* it" — should be considered both premise and conclusion to the other ten. It summarizes, in a profundity that shakes the foundations of bourgeois liberalist practice, Marx's radical alternative to interpretivism and philosophers as interpreters of reality.

Marx's critical revolution against Hegel had as its basis that philosophy was based in a false practice of the labor process. Abstraction from real interests, objective activity, and self-objectification through labor led philosophy to define knowledge production in terms of abstract labor, namely, abstract thought. The basis for arriving at philosophical certainty and truth consisted in specifying the properties, rules, logic, and methods abstract thought should follow in order to create the rational basis for truthful inquiry.

When Marx says "the point is to *change* it," he is not expressing mere outrage at the world; rather, Marx is here claiming that philosophy cannot know reality since knowledge, *real* knowledge, cannot be produced in abstraction from the process of *making* reality. The objective activity of labor must replace the practice of "intellectual," "theoretical," or merely speculative labor. This is *not* a statement about the morality of revolutionary activity; nor is it a stance that merely furnishes theoretical labor with a practical agenda. This consequence of transforming the very basis of truth-making activity from intellectual labor to the process of self-objectification more generally revolutionizes the very meaning of knowledge.

This alternative practice of the labor process does not suggest that some atheoretical immediacy of "the here and now" is the basis for revolutionary strategy. It does mean, however, that the real truth of history is to be sought in the process of its objectification through labor, and therefore, the making-changing of reality through labor is truthful activity.

The other ten theses ground Marx's eleventh by fleshing out the very terms of objective activity in the form of a critique of non-Marxist materialism. That staid, abstract individual of bourgeois society—the grounding of Feuerbachian materialism and Wright's sociologism—is replaced with Marx's argument concerning the practice of subjectivity as *objective* activity. It would be a grave mistake to claim that Marx's critique has in fact led to the abandonment of this bourgeois liberalist premise, even by so-called Marxists. The bourgeois social formation producing alienated practices of the knowledge production process itself must be revolutionized in practice.

In conclusion, class analysis as revolutionizing nontextual objectification must have as its grounding the real labor process. The meaning of class is the making of class; the objectivity of class relations, class formation and class struggle resides in the process of self-objectification, not in some abstract 'conceptual object' of sociologized Marxism. Marxism was never meant to be subsumed to the bourgeois horizons and grounding of present-day academic sociology. And the question of the future of sociologized Marxism certainly raises the prospects and possibilities for renewed debate over Marx's meaning.

It is most certainly the case that since the historical-institutional practice of Marxism within the present social formation of social sciences has mostly shaped the terrain for the construction of much sociologized class analysis, this project will remain an insurgent one. In fact, to my surprise some of the most staunch defenders of the present practice of social science were to be found among persons practicing a Marxism from within the social sciences. The attempt to construct an alternative practice of class analysis that radically challenges the conventional social-scientific practice of knowledge production (and its premise in abstract labor) has among its enemies many Marxists who see no other way to practice Marxism. On the other hand, this is not surprising, since the battles to establish Marxism as a real historical competitor to bourgeois science is being fought *within* bourgeois science. One of the most common practices to come out of this battle, however, is the abandonment of a Marxist practice of the labor process and the practice of Marxism as a mere variant of bourgeois grounded theory (i.e. Marxist vs. non-Marxist *sociological* theory).

The strategic-political reality confronting all those who currently labor-work within academic sociology may prevent the transforming of present-day sociologized Marxism into a real Marxist sociology. Practicing class analysis as the process of self-objectification within and through the process of revolutionary class formation and class struggle is certainly not the quickest way to academic notoriety, merit pay, or accolades. Creating the basis for revolutionary class formation is a far cry from hiding behind the methodological canons of bourgeois social theory.

Marxist class analysis is not a variant of neo-Kantian sociology, and as such a sociology, is incapable of producing the strategic-political grounding for revolutionizing reality. Class analysis must itself be internal to the labor process — not as abstract labor constructing "the concept of class" but as revolutionary workers making class objective. It is not merely a question of theory versus practice. Marx has eliminated the false practice of labor that allowed their separation in the first place, namely, the abstraction of the subject from the process of making reality through labor. It is about a new practice, a new sociology, a new Marxism that challenges the very concept builders and boundary hunters who turn class into its idea. And the idea, of course, is that special product uniquely facilitated by those well practiced in the science of metaphysics, without which, revolutionizing practice would most certainly benefit.

Notes

1. At a recent panel discussion on Wright's book *Classes,* held as part of the annual meeting of the American Sociological Association in Chicago, August 1987, it was amazing to witness the spectacle of "Marxists" unwilling to admit that Wright was indeed grounded in neoclassical economics and Weberian sociology. It took Arthur Stinchcombe, one who has been implicated in Wright's project from his earliest days at Berkeley (1973-76), to make this very basic point.
2. This is another example where Marxism is read through a neo-Kantian sociology. Hence, dialectics is transformed into a standard sociological claim vis-á-vis interaction between sociological variables. While interaction would certainly undermine Wright's empirical investigation, it is no substitute for a Marxist dialectic.
3. G.W.F. Hegel was of outstanding significance for Marx's practice of the labor process. Marx's acknowledgment of Hegel's argument on objectification and the production of meaning in society is explicitly cited, for example, in the 1844 *Manuscripts.*

> The outstanding achievement of Hegel's *Phanomenologie* and of its final outcome, the dialectic of negativity as the moving and generating principle, is thus first that Hegel conceives the self-creation of man as a process, conceives objectification as loss of the object, as alienation and as transcendence of this alienation; that he thus grasps the essence of *labour* and comprehends objective man—true, because real man—as the outcome of man's *own labour.* (Marx and Engels 1975, 333.)

While Hegel posited the necessity and actuality of labor as the basis for objectification, Marx vociferously criticized Hegel and the Hegelians for their abstract philosophical practice of objectification. Objective activity is not, as Hegelianism argued, based in the abstract speculative labor of philosophical thinking. As Marx claimed, "For Hegel the *human being—*

man — equals *self-consciousness.* All estrangement of the human being is therefore *nothing* but *estrangement of self consciousness"* (ibid., 334). As Marx further remarks, Hegel's premise of philosophical labor implicates his entire self-understanding of objectification. "The only labour which Hegel knows and recognizes is *abstractly mental* labour. Therefore, that which constitutes the *essence* of philosophy — the *alienation of man who knows himself,* or *alienated* science *thinking itself* — Hegel grasps as its essence" (ibid., 333).

4. My focus on the 1844 *Manuscripts* for reconstructing Marx's critique of Hegelian dialectic is based on the fact that it is in these manuscripts that Marx forcefully and fundamentally critiques Hegel at the level of his basic grounding. There are other works (e.g. *Contribution to the Critique of Hegel's Philosophy of Right, On the Jewish Question, The Holy Family or Critique of Critical Criticism, The German Ideology,* and *The Poverty of Philosophy)* where Marx critizes Hegel directly or indirectly through Young Hegelianism, but none approaches the depth and breadth of revolutionizing critique to be found in the *Manuscripts.*

5. Harry Cleaver (1979) has been immensely useful for this stage of my argument. The strategy of "reading *Capital* politically," as opposed to idealistically as political economy or philosophy, serves as the basis for grounding a dialectic of labor directly in the class relation.

6. See (Marx 1967, 49). Also, see Marx's (1983) letter to Engels of August 24, 1867 where he claims: ". . . the best thing about my book is 1.(on this rests the *entire* comprehension of the facts) the *two-fold character of labour,* whether it is expressed in use-value or exchange- value, which is emphasized right in the first chapter. . ."

7. Letter of Marx to Engels, April 2, 1858 in Marx (1983).

8. The *Theses on Feuerbach* were in fact entitled "ad Feuerbach" by Marx and were made textually available in edited form posthumously in an appendix to Engels's (1888) pamphlet *Ludwig Feuerbach and the End of Classical German Philosophy.* By then, however, the revolutionary meaning of the criticisms of Feuerbach by Marx was being practiced through Engels's naturalistically based scientific method, revitalized Kantianism within Germany, and the non-Marxist materialisms of the Second International. Marx's own early writings were not available, while Engels's quickly replaced Marx's as the basis for authoritative Marxist philosophy. For an excellent account of how Marxism had been fundamentally "revised" by the time of the latter nineteenth century and for all practical purposes official Marxisms have developed doctrines ungrounded in Marx's own arguments-practices, see Colletti (1974, 7-18).

REFERENCES

Althusser, Louis. 1969. *For Marx.* London: Allen Lane, Penguin.

Althusser, Louis, and Etienne Balibar. 1970. *Reading Capital.* London: New Left Books.

_____. 1976. *Essays in Self Criticism.* London: New Left Books.

Anderson, Perry. 1976. *Considerations in Western Marxism.* London: New Left Books.

_____. 1980. *Debates within English Marxism.* London: New Left Books.

Andrew, Edward. 1983. "Class in Itself and Class Against Capital: Karl Marx and His Classifiers." *Canadian Journal of Political Science* 16(3) (September): 577-584.

Avineri, Shlomo. 1968. *The Social and Political Thought of Karl Marx.* Cambridge: Cambridge University Press.

Benton, Ted. 1984. *The Rise and Fall of Structuralist Marxism: Althusser and His Influence.* New York: St. Martin's Press.

Bottomore, Tom, and Paul Goode, eds. 1983. *Readings in Marxist Sociology.* New York: Oxford University Press.

Burawoy, Michael. 1982. "The Resurgence of Marxism in American Sociology." Special Supplement. *American Journal of Sociology.*

_____. 1986. Book review essay, "Making Nonsense out of Marx." *Contemporary Sociology,* (September) 15(5): 704-707.

Callinicos, Alex. 1976. *Althusser's Marxism.* London.

161

Carling, Alan. 1986. "Rational Choice Marxism." *New Left Review,* no. 160 (November/December).

Cleaver, Harry. 1979. *Reading 'Capital' Politically.* Austin: University of Texas Press.

Colletti, Lucio. 1974. "Introduction" to *Karl Marx: Early Writings.* New York: Vintage.

Elster, Jon. 1982. "Marxism, Functionalism and Game Theory: The Case for Methodological Individualism." *Theory and Society,* July, 453-482.

————. 1985. *Making Sense of Marx.* Cambridge: Cambridge University Press.

Geras, Norman. 1972. "Althusser's Marxism: An Account and Assessment." *New Left Review,* no. 71, 57-86.

Glucksmann, A. 1972. "A Ventriloquist Structuralism." *New Left Review.* no. 160, 68-92.

Gramsci, Antonio. 1971. *Selections from Prison Notebooks,* ed. and trans. Quintin Hoare and G.N. Smith. New York: International Publishers.

Hegel, G.W.F. 1969. *Science of Logic,* trans. Miller. London: Allen and Unwin.

Kant, Immanuel. 1929. *Critique of Pure Reason,* trans. Norman Kemp Smith. New York: St. Martin's Press.

Keat, Russell, and John Urry. 1982. *Social Theory as Science.* 2d ed. London: Routledge and Kegan Paul.

Levine, Andrew. 1984. *Arguing for Socialism.* London: Routledge and Kegan Paul.

Lukacs, Georg. 1971. *History and Class Consciousness.* Cambridge, Mass.: MIT Press.

Marx, Karl. 1967. *Capital,* vol. 1. New York: International Publishers.

————. 1973. *Grundrisse,* trans. Martin Nicolaus. 1st Vintage ed. The Marx Library. New York: Vintage.

————. 1983. *Letters on 'Capital',* trans. Drummond. London: New Park Publications.

Marx, K., and F. Engels. 1975. *Collected Works*. vols. 1, 3. Moscow: Progress Publishers.

_____. 1976. *Collected Works,* vol. 5. Moscow: Progress Publishers.

McLellan, David. 1979. *Marxism after Marx: An Introduction.* Boston: Houghton Mifflin.

_____, ed. 1983 *Marx: The First Hundred Years.* London: F. Pinter in association with Fontana Books.

Ollman, Bertell, and Edward Vernoff eds. 1982. *The Left Academy: Marxist Scholarship on American Campuses.* New York: McGraw-Hill.

Plekhanov, Georgy. 1969. *Fundamental Problems of Marxism.* New York: International Publishers.

Poulantzas, Nicos. 1973. *Political Power and Social Classes.* London: New Left Books.

Przeworski, Adam. 1977. "Proletariat into a Class: The Process of Class Formation from Karl Kautsky's *The Class Struggle* to Recent Controversies." *Politics and Society* 7(4):343-401.

_____. 1982. "The Ethical Materialism of John Roemer." *Politics and Society* 11(3):289-313.

Roemer, John. 1981. *Analytic Foundations of Marxian Economic Theory.* New York: Cambridge University Press.

_____. 1982a. *A General Theory of Exploitation and Class.* Cambridge, Mass.: Harvard University Press.

_____. 1982b. "Methodological Individualism and Deductive Marxism." *Theory and Society* 11 (July) :513-520.

Rorty, Richard. 1979. *Philosophy and the Mirror of Nature.* Princeton: Princeton University Press.

Schmidt, Alfred. 1981. *History and Structure: An Essay on the Hegelian-Marxist and Structuralist Theories of History.* Cambridge, Mass.: MIT Press.

Taylor, Charles. 1975. *Hegel.* Cambridge: Cambridge University Press.

_____. 1979. *Hegel and Modern Society.* Cambridge: Cambridge University Press.

Thompson, E.P. 1978. *The Poverty of Theory*. London: Merlin Press.

Vilar, Pierre. 1973. "Marxist History, a History in the Making: Toward a Dialogue with Althusser." *New Left Review,* no. 80.

Wood, Ellen Meiksins. 1986. *The Retreat from Class: A New "True" Socialism.* London: Verso.

Wright, Erik Olin. 1963. "Response to Auditory Stimulus in the Developing Rat." *Transactions of the Kansas Academy of Sciences* 66(2).

_____. 1964. "Analysis of the Total Number of Twists Resulting from Cutting Any Order Moebius Band with Any Number of Cuts." *Transactions of the Kansas Academy of Sciences* 67(2).

_____. 1973. "A Study of Student Leaves of Absence." *Journal of Higher Education* 44(3).

_____. 1976a. "Class Boundaries in Advanced Capitalist Societies." *New Left Review,* no. 98 (July-August): 3-41.

_____. 1976b. "Modes of Class Struggle and the Capitalist State." *Kapitalistate,* no. 4, 186-220.

_____. 1977. "Marxist Class Categories and Income Inequality." *American Sociological Review.* 42(1):32-55.

_____. 1978a. "Race, Class and Income Inequality." *American Journal of Sociology* May, 368-397.

_____. 1978b. "Intellectuals and the Working Class." *Insurgent Sociologist.* (Winter) 8(1): 5-18.

_____. 1979a. *Class, Crisis and the State.* London: New Left Books.

_____. 1979b. *Class Structure and Income Determination.* New York: Academic Press.

_____. 1982. "The Status of the Political in the Concept of Class Structure." *Politics and Society, 11(3):321-341.*

_____. *1983a. "Giddens' Critique of Marxism." New Left Review,* no. 138 (March-April) :11-35.

————. 1983b. "What Is Marxist and What Is Neo- in Neo-Marxist Class Analysis?" Manuscript.

————. 1983-84. "The Theory and Methodology of Marxist Social Science." *Syllabus for SOC 621-622.*

————. 1984. "A General Framework for the Analysis of Class Structure." *Politics and Society* 13(4):383-423.

————. 1985a. *Curriculum Vitae.* September.

————. 1985b. *Classes.* London: Verso.

————. 1987. "Towards a Post-Marxist Radical Social Theory." Book review essay of Bowles and Gintis, *Democracy and Capitalism: Property, Community, and the Contradictions of Modern Social Thought . Contemporary Sociology.* 16(5) (September): 748-753.

Wright, Erik Olin, et al., 1982. "The American Class Structure." *American Sociological Review* 47 (December): 709-726

Index